The

HOME BAR BASICS

(and not-so-basics)

OVER 200 ESSENTIAL RECIPES FOR

Slings & Sours, Grogs & Nogs

DAVE STOLTE
with
JASON SCHIFFER

Thanks to Eric Alperin, Anu Apte, Payman Bahmani, Zahra Bates, Michelle Bearden, Jeff Berry, Greg Boehm, Richie Boccato, Chris Bostick, Joe Brooke, Jared Brown, Brooke Cannons, Dave Castillo, Erick Castro, Martin Cate, Toby Cecchini, Paul Clarke, Shaun Cole, Jennifer Colliau, Forrest Cokely, Danielle Crouch, Wayne Curtis, Dale DeGroff, Gabrielle Dion, Daniel Djang, Ron Dollete, Beau DuBois, Trevor Easter, Matt Ellingson, Camper English, Tomas Estes, H.E. Greer, Jacob Grier, Cari Hah, Ed Hamilton, Paul Harrington, Eric Johnson, Allan Katz, Joe Keeper, Mindy Kucan, Steven Liles, Jake Lustig, Anne Louise Marquis, Paul McGee, Chris McMillian, Jim Meehan, Kelly Merrell, Jeffrey Morgenthaler, Matej Novak, Chris Patino, Mike Reis, Blair Reynolds, Dänny Ronen, Matt Robold, Anthony Schmidt, David Shenaut, Ria Soler, Chuck Taggart, Devon Tarby, and David Wondrich for sharing their candid, keen, and boozy wisdom with me over the years. To Jason, Nick, and Katie for your constant inspiration and hope. And to Kristin for your love, support, friendship, and patience with the condition of the kitchen. "I'll get it in the morning!"

— Dave

GAZ REGAN | ROCKY YEH
IN MEMORIAM

Published in the United States of America by Wexler of California

Printed in the United States of America

Third edition, December 2020
homebarbasics.com
facebook.com/homebarbasics
instagram.com/homebarbasics

Enjoy responsibly. Don't go too far.

WELCOME

10 years ago, I noticed an empty space on the home bartender's bookshelf. To the left were all the great trailblazing books of the late 19th- and early 20th-century, along with a handful from the emerging craft scene of the 1990s. To the right were an enthusiastic new crop of books, hardbacks full of stunning photography and equally stunning (read: unattainable) recipes. But that spot in the middle? The practical little pocket book that brings home the keys to the craft cocktail revolution? It didn't exist. So I did my best to help fill that gap. The first two editions of *Home Bar Basics (and Not-So-Basics)* came and went, but I haven't stopped learning about drinks, refining my techniques, and broadening my approach. My good friend Jason Schiffer, a career bartender and restaurateur, was with me every sip of the way on that journey and I'm grateful he's joined me as co-author on this round, helping redefine central concepts, improve recipes, detail techniques, and solidify brand recommendations. But enough of that. I'm glad you're here. What can I get you?

Dave Stolte

BACK TO BASICS

When I started bartending in the 1990s, my bosses required me to memorize 350 recipes before they'd let me serve guests. There was no system — just a long list. So I organized the recipes into groups, simply to help me learn them. And it worked. Later, as I discovered and joined the craft cocktail revolution, I began to learn about drink families and their histories. When I became a restaurant owner, I was on better footing to teach recipes and techniques to my bartenders. Gathering and building on what many other industry professionals have shared, I streamlined how these drink families work. Simplicity and elegance are things I like to experience in cocktails. The "Basics," those drinks that really stand the test of time, they shine due to their effortless confidence. When we move to those "Not-So-Basics," we build on the backbone of each family, using new or unlikely flavor pairings and finding new ways to enjoy them. I'm stoked that Dave brought me along to share these ideas with you, and I hope you're inspired to learn more.

Jason Schiffer

HOSPITALITY: THE ANGLE

There's a lot to explore in 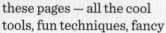 these pages — all the cool tools, fun techniques, fancy bottles, and delicious flavors... but I'd be remiss if I didn't let you know my position up front: Taking care of yourself and your guests is the primary consideration. Even more than making great drinks, *being a great host* is what allows folks to have a good time and demonstrates that you care about them. Hospitality simply means doing your best to make sure everyone is welcome, comfortable, entertained, satisfied, and safe.

When hosting guests, start with a bit of self-care: Keep things manageable by narrowing the focus of your offerings beforehand. You could even write up a menu with a handful of suggested drinks to help your guests navigate the options — this approach also ensures you have time beforehand to prep any ingredients you might need. Be prepared for those who might just want beer or wine, a simple Vodka Soda, or neat whiskey. Set out plenty of nonalcoholic options for designated drivers and those who don't partake. Make water easily accessible and plentiful to encourage hydration between every alcoholic drink ("detox before you retox"). Always offer food with drinks, even if it's just a simple bowl of nuts. For gatherings of more than six, you might consider a bowl of punch, a pitcher of sangria (with more ready in the fridge), or a host of other batched offerings adaptable to large groups (see the index for a full list of ideas). Faced with a large gathering and one hour notice one time, I just poured one bottle each of Campari, Italian vermouth, and Prosecco over ice in a punch bowl: a large-format Negroni Sbagliato, an instant party. Isn't it more fun to hang out with your friends than it is to be supplying custom drink requests all night? Relax and have a drink or two with them, but lead by example and don't go too far. If things do get hectic with drinkmaking, recruit a friend to act as your "barback," helping out with cleaning up and keeping the flow going.

Do your best to keep an eye on guests who may have become overserved, and help steer them toward safety by securing a safe ride home with a sober friend or a ridesharing service. Keep hospitality in mind without getting overly fussy, take care of yourself, and your gatherings will always be a hit.

A SPIRITED TIME MACHINE

The history of boozing demonstrates everything smart and everything stupid about humanity. As an early people, we noticed the natural process of fermentation: living microorganisms transforming carbs into alcohol and sugars into ethanol. We eventually learned to manage fermentation to make amazing things like bread, beer, cider, and wine (then later cheese, pickles, and hot sauce, among others) in a form of controlled decay that made certain foods more digestible while reducing waste and spoilage. On a separate track farther along, figuring out the magic of distillation enabled our forebears to purify water, to create medicine and perfumes from plants... and to use fermented beverages to make distilled spirits for a pleasurable change of mind. We eventually figured out that spirits are also fatally toxic (short-term and long-term) — outside of moderation — and potentially addictive. So the story here is about creativity, ingenuity, and resourcefulness, but also about our own inherent tendencies to self-sabotage. With beverage alcohol, we've certainly created a delicious monster, one that can serve us better if we approach it with respect and awareness.

Fermented low-alcoholic beverages were enjoyed for thousands of years as a primary method of hydration, since water was prone to contamination. Wine originated in China about 7000 BCE and was originally consumed as a delivery vehicle for medicinal herbs, not enjoyed on its own — think of it as the world's first vermouth. Mead may have been enjoyed in China about the same period as wine, spreading to India by 1700 BCE and Scotland by 500 BCE. The origins of pulque (the fermented, milky sap of ripe agaves) in Mexico appear to occur as early as 5000 BCE, around the same time that beermaking was documented on Egyptian papyrus scrolls. Wine arrived in the Mediterranean and the Middle East between 5000 and 4000 BCE. The Celtic people in England made a rough cider around 3000 BCE and trendy kombucha, the lightly-alcoholic fermented tea, came later — around 200 BCE in China. In that world of limited knowledge where people only had access to locally-available resources, overcoming the spoilage factor became essential: this is where distillation enters the picture.

Distillation is, in simplest terms, the process of removing substances from a liquid via boiling and condensation. For example, distilling sea water separates salt. Distilling fresh water removes bacteria, minerals, and other impurities. Skillful distilling of fermented materials removes toxic methanol while focusing and creating flavors. The first known distillation devices, alembic stills, were invented in China, the Mediterranean, and modern-day Iraq between 1200 BCE and 800 CE by chemists looking to condense mercury, make ceremonial elixirs, and just generally unlock the secrets of the universe. There's compelling evidence of ceramic pot stills being used in southern Mexico around 500 BCE, but widespread distillation in the Americas didn't happen until much later, when European colonizers brought the practice with them. By 830 CE, Arab chemists and their counterparts in China (around 900 CE) figured out how to distill medicinal and beverage spirits from wine and rosewater, making the first eau-de-vie. This name (from the Latin "aqua vitae," meaning "water of life") has persisted in modern usage: the Gaelic translation "uisce

beatha" has evolved to become "whiskey," the Scandinavian "aquavit," and even the Polish "okowita" that later became "wódka."

 We see the first specialized beverage spirits between 1100 and 1270: arak in Persia, proto-amari in Italy, uisce beatha in Ireland and Scotland, and baijiu in China. The more widespread creation and consumption of diverse local spirits happened alongside the Old World's emergence from the Dark Ages during the Age of Exploration. Between 1450 and 1650, there was a creative surge in larger-scale distillation for sale or trade, with mezcal in Mexico, aguardiente in Brazil and the Caribbean, cognac in France, and rum in Barbados. During this period, distilled beverage alcohol made from a variety of locally-available and newly-imported foodstuffs became common throughout the world — primarily as a way to consume infused medicinal plants, but also thought of as a health tonic in its own right, apart from the botanicals. It wasn't until the 1700s that the culture around drinking spirits for fun became a thing. And oof, it took off in a big, not-so-fun way. People didn't understand the damage booze could do: The gin craze in 1730s England wreaked havoc in London with widespread addiction, violence, and social devastation. As the pace of life accelerated and people began to get their heads around the concept of moderation, the practice of communal punch bowl imbibing in England and Colonial America gave way to the rise of single serve mixed drinks, many of which we still enjoy today in forms that would've been familiar to our ancestors: an Old Fashioned, Mojito, or Egg Nog would not be out of place if you were to time travel. In a way, every time we enjoy a cocktail, we're staying connected to our shared history.

COCKTAIL TIME

What we think of today as "cocktails" have a scattered here-and-there timeline. Could we call that early Chinese wine infused with botanicals, maybe sweetened with mead a "cocktail" by today's thinking? What about the rough aguardiente Sir Francis Drake mixed with raw sugar, fresh limes, and mint — or the spiced proto-Egg Nog enjoyed in Medieval England? They all sound like cocktails to me. Many regard 1800 as the point when modern thinking about cocktails begins with the debut of the Whiskey Cocktail: a style of drink they called a "bittered sling" composed of spirit, sugar, bitters, and dilution. Sound familiar? It was in the United States  that the practice of combining different ingredients from different cultures reached its enthusiastic culinary zenith, mirroring our "melting pot" sales pitch. As the 1800s marched on, we saw the rise of the Sour family, downsizing the large-format punch into a focused little flavor bomb that fits in your hand. The availability of ice, the creation of specialty bartending tools

 during the Industrial Age, and the import of European liqueurs and vermouths inspired bartenders in all the major metros to create enduring classics. The Golden Age of Cocktails flourished from 1860 to 1920, when it all came crashing down during national Prohibition. An array of products ceased to exist and skilled career bartenders at the top of their game suddenly found themselves out of work — forcing retirement, a change of trade, or relocation to places where they'd be appreciated, like Paris, London, and Venice. A funny thing happened with Prohibition: it didn't eliminate evil from the face of the land as intended.

Irksome to its proponents, Prohibition forced drinking underground. Men and women began to drink together in social settings, and people of different genetic and cultural backgrounds co-mingled, listening to that devil jazz music and even smoking the reefer. Say it ain't so! As the United States emerged from Prohibition, an enterprising hustler who called himself "Don the Beachcomber," facing the loss of varied liqueurs and a glut of cheap rum, took it upon himself to roll his own: He created multiple original syrups and "dimensionalized" previously simple drinks like the Daiquiri and the Planter's Punch to single-handedly kickstart the tropical drinks craze that flowed through the 1960s. But the shadow of Prohibition tainted American drinking all the way until the 1990s, when a handful of curious bartenders like Dale DeGroff, Gaz Regan, Paul Harrington, and Audrey Saunders wondered how things were done back when bartenders gave a shit about quality and their craft — "celebrating spirits instead of hiding them," as California distiller Lance Winters has said. They pioneered the resurgence of cocktail-making as a vital part of the American culinary landscape, inspired countless bartenders to blaze new trails.

We even saw the return of products that hadn't seen broad (or any) distribution in 75 years, like orange bitters, rye whiskey, and crème de violette. Thoughtful craft distillers are now making some of the best spirits the world has seen, while thankfully many old-guard brands have stood the test of time with renewed respect. It's safe to say the Cocktail Revolution has been won in favor of the cocktail, and in favor of us. Flavored vodka is on the wane. Struggles to get a decent Old Fashioned are no more. Previously ignored or under-represented groups now have a respected voice in the conversation. As far as cocktail culture goes, the good old days are now. Where we stand at this point seems to be a bit of a "what next?" moment. Only time will tell.

MEET THE FAMILIES

The drinks in this book are organized into four families, defined by their key characteristics. This is just one way of imposing order on the chaotic and sprawling world of cocktails. For example, some might group cars by color or fuel type, categorize animals by habitat or kingdom... one way is not The Way. This is simply my way. I think it makes sense.

SLINGS are spirit-forward mixed drinks, typically balanced with sweetness and aromatics (botanical elements that can veer from bitter to floral: think baking spices, citrus oils, and dried roots). These drinks are built or stirred — methods that will be discussed in detail in the red-bordered Techniques section.

SOURS find spirit balanced with sweetness and some form of acid, usually citrus juice. This family is where we discover the "heart of tartness." Shaking, not stirring, is the rule. They can be served up or down (see the back-flap glossary for these terms).

GROGS are lengthened with more dilution than booze: think seltzer, various sodas, coffee, and such. What they call "quaffable" on a hot day (or hot grogs for cold days). Mostly water, light and easy. Even easier — they're usually built right in the glass.

NOGS are thickened with milk, heavy cream, egg, coconut, even ice cream. Rich and indulgent, they are comfort drinks at brunch, for dessert, or any occasion when one needs a treat. Nogs require a rousing shake.

THE BASICS VS. THE NOT-SO-BASICS

Admittedly, in this book, The Not-So-Basics far outweigh The Basics in terms of quantity. But The Basics certainly prevail when it comes to significance. As you read, you'll see **The Basics** called out in red: a diverse collection of recipes, techniques, ingredients, preparations, and gear that form the core of a home bartender's skill set. For quick-reference convenience, I've collected all The Basic drinks and kit components on the inside front cover.

Ingredients and **Gear** are detailed in the Stocking Up section (no worries if you see something unusual in a recipe, like dried horehound or xanthan gum, there's a list of online resources in the index). Ahead of diving in to the recipes, you'll learn the essential **Techniques** for proper shaking, stirring, and more. **Recipes** for Slings & Sours, Grogs & Nogs feature cornerstone examples of their families, with similar recipes organized nearby in a "browsing order" to encourage exploration and discover connections. The last section of the book details homemade **Preparations** like syrups, cordials, liqueurs, and more. **The Not-So-Basics** occupy the bulk of the book across all sections: Here you'll achieve altitude by expanding on your foundational knowledge. Swap one ingredient and the entire character of a drink changes, or take the technique for making a basic syrup and apply it to making cordials. The more comfortable you get in the kitchen, the more opportunities there are for you to go deeper. I hope this approach encourages you to add skills and gain the confidence to create your own original drinks.

STOCKING UP

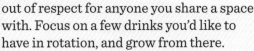

It's tempting to go wild and load up on everything. I advise you to build your home bar inventory slowly: for the sake of your budget, to give yourself time to develop and learn, and out of respect for anyone you share a space with. Focus on a few drinks you'd like to have in rotation, and grow from there.

Your collection of **GEAR** is an investment. Look for the best-quality tools you can afford (although quality isn't always expensive). No sense in buying something flimsy that doesn't work well and winds up breaking after a while. Design-wise, there are enough products available now that you can, if you choose to, build a set of tools that reflects your own style, becoming functional *and* decorative elements in your home. Bar tools should work and delight, never frustrate. The **jigger** you select needs a two-ounce capacity on one side and a one-ounce capacity on the other, with some kind of clear, graduated marks indicating varying volumes, like three-quarters or one and a half ounces. Ergonomically, it should feel good in your hand, easy to flip from one side to the other single-handedly, not tip over when rested on the counter, and be of sturdy construction. Your **barspoon** should also feel balanced and elegant in your hand, substantial but not heavy. Look for one that's a single-piece construction (tacked-on pieces tend to break off) with a smoothly-rounded or twisted stem that enables a gliding spin when you stir. Note: a barspoon is not a unit of measure — the bowls of these spoons are rarely calibrated, so you'll be need a set of standard **measuring spoons** when preparing drinks. Find a **mixing glass** that's somewhat heavy with a thick bottom — this will help insulate and chill the drink, giving you the best control over dilution. Straight, smooth, vertical walls are the standard for ease of stirring. I've tried all kinds of shakers: Boston, cobbler, and Parisian — glass, metal, plastic, and insulated. I recommend the same kind used by most professional craft bartenders: a **two-piece "tin on tin" shaker**, with one larger "Boston" tin and a smaller "cheater" tin, as they call it. Look for tins with sturdy weighted bottoms for balance when shaking, and purchase them as a set to ensure they fit together snugly. When you first start using them, they'll be somewhat rigid, but as you break them in, the metal will become more flexible and accommodating, creating a tighter seal. For straining, use a **Hawthorne strainer**: It ingeniously employs a spring on the interior, so it becomes adaptable to a range of differently-sized vessels, while the spring helps catch ice and other materials from the shaker. By sliding the top plate of the strainer down towards the serving glass as you pour, you can catch additional smaller bits that might slip through the spring in an action called "closing the gate." For straining stirred drinks, you can use the Hawthorne or the traditional, old-fashioned **julep strainer**, essentially a large perforated spoon that rests in the mixing glass with the rounded side down to hold ice in place while you pour. A conical

fine-mesh strainer further assists with straining drinks on occasion, but is also handy for straining pulp and seeds from freshly-squeezed juice. Speaking of which, you'll want an **elbow juicer** for limes and a **reamer** for lemons and oranges (the kind with a collection dish is handy). A straight vegetable peeler or (my preference) a **Y-peeler** is essential for making citrus twists. If you don't have a **muddler**, the end of a large wooden spoon will suffice, but like a true **swizzle stick** (a trimmed branch of the Caribbean *Quararibea turbinata* tree), some tools have value just in being esoteric conversation starters. Reliable, cold seltzer is always on hand with an **iSi Soda Siphon**. A reliable **electric blender** will expand your options year-round for making tropical drinks, frozen Margaritas, and homemade Egg Nog (among others). I like eight-ounce squirt-top **condiment bottles** with attached caps for syrups and cordials, name- and date-labeled with a **Dymo labeler**. Bamboo or metal **cocktail picks** are essential for certain garnishes, as is a **microplane** for grating nutmeg, chocolate, and coffee. A **mister** is an easy way to coat a glass interior or accent the surface of a drink with absinthe or other components.

Keep compostable corn **straws** handy for those who ask — a smart, sustainable choice. A **nut milk bag** or cheesecloth is essential for straining some preparations. Standard kitchen items like a **sharp knife** (serrated also works for citrus), **cutting board**, **measuring cups**, **bottle opener**, **corkscrew**, **sieve**, and coffee or **spice grinder** round out your kit.

GLASSWARE, literally and figuratively, serves the drink. Each shape has a purpose behind its form, from stems and punch sets to highballs and lowballs. The eight- to 10-ounce **rocks** glass should have a hefty bottom to help insulate the drink. The **double rocks** glass holds 10 to 13 ounces and is primarily used for tropical drinks that come served with a fair amount of pebble ice. The elegant five-and-a-half ounce **coupe** has made a welcome return as the standard for craft drinks served up, replacing the V-shaped, so-called "Martini" glasses of the '90s that grew to ridiculous proportions, slopping their drinks over the side the whole time. Tall glasses, made to prevent bubbles from escaping too quickly, come in four sizes: the short eight-ounce **fizz**, the 10-ounce

highball, the 11-ounce **Collins**, and the 13 ½-ounce **chimney** or Zombie glass. You'll get double-duty from a six-ounce **Georgian** glass for hot and cold drinks. A 12- to 15-ounce **snifter** is called for by a couple of tropical drinks and frozen drinks. A vintage set of **punch bowl & cups with ladle** is a bargain at thrift stores. **Tiki mugs** can be a fun and frivolous way to serve mid-century tropical drinks. There are some great creative artisans producing new mugs that avoid the problematic stereotypes of some vintage designs. Pewter **julep cups** are beautiful and create a protective frost around your Mint Juleps. Ensure your julep cups are food-grade: some are made for decorative uses only. Footed **pilsner** glasses will work for the beer of the same name, plus some cocktails — speaking of beer, you'll want **tulip** and **pint** glasses for other styles. For wine, use both **Burgundy** and **white wine** glasses; a few **champagne flutes** ensure elegance is always available. Shot glasses like the tall **caballito** and the votive-inspired **veladora** encourage sipping rather than shooting. Look for all these glasses online, at restaurant-supply stores, or at thrift stores and vintage shops.

Overcoming "the **ICE** problem" is consistently the single largest factor that can affect a home bartender's drink quality. What's the problem, exactly? The answer lies in understanding the nature and purpose of ice in preparing and serving drinks. Without getting too far down a rabbit hole, the more clear your ice is, the slower it will dilute, the sturdier it will be when shaking, and, to be honest, the prettier it will be. "We drink with our eyes first," the saying goes. At home, people usually employ ice trays or built-in icemakers that make crescent-shaped "cubes" that are afflicted with every problem you don't want your cocktail ice to have: cloudiness from trapped air and dissolved minerals, off-flavors from freezing and being stored next to food items, softness, and ugliness. Quality bars and restaurants have large, dedicated ice machines as part of their essential equipment: usually a Kold-Draft or a Hoshizaki for ice cubes and a Scotsman for pebble ice. Higher-end craft bars may have custom-cut, perfectly-clear ice delivered, or even have their own ice house out back with the seriously hardcore Clinebell, a machine originally made for producing the kind of ice that ends up carved in the shape of a swan at special events. These crystalline, 300-pound blocks can also be cut down for cocktail use to make large rocks, Collins spears, and cubes. Home bartenders simply don't have that kind of luxury. In a standard freezer, water solidifies from the outside toward the inside, trapping cloudiness in the center. The secret to clear ice is changing the orientation of this "directional freezing" — by insulating the vessel and slowing down the process, water is forced to freeze from the top to the bottom, where cloudiness can be separated. Writer and researcher Camper English has led the quality ice movement with home-scale experiments that mimic the Clinebell's method. His website is listed in the Resources section if you choose to go that way — with either a DIY rig or a commercial product. Another option, rather than making your own, is to purchase a 25-pound "clear" block from your local ice house. I say "clear" because there will be cloudiness at the center, but if you let the ice soften up a bit — 20 or 30 minutes — you can use a serrated bread knife to carve the block into large, clear ice cubes that rival the best craft bars, while discarding the cloudy parts and saving scraps for shaking. Placing the ice block on an inverted sheet pan with a dishtowel under the ice introduces a bit of bounce into the carving that helps ensure straight cuts. Yes, this sounds obsessive, and for many of you this is overkill and no fun. So we'll detail below best practices for working with cloudy ice if that's all you have. Sorry, I know that sounds judgy. It's a tough world in Ice Land, kiddo.

Block Ice is used in punch bowls, roughly 6″ x 6″ x 4″ or whatever size is appropriate for your bowl, leaving enough room on its sides for the ladle to do its thing.

 Rock Ice is used in Slings like the Old Fashioned and Negroni: spirit-forward slow-sippers that benefit from gradual dilution. Form rock ice using a directional-freezing icemaker or hand carve it down from a block to fit snugly in your Rocks glass without extending too far beyond the height of the rim. It should make good contact with the bottom of the glass to help conduct cold.

Ice Cubes should stack easily into a glass, and despite the name, they don't necessarily have to be perfectly cubic. You'll use ice cubes for Highballs and Collinses, but also for shaking. Form them using a directional-freezing icemaker or hand carve down from larger rocks.

Pebble Ice isn't something you can carve unless you've gone over to the backside of sanity... in which case you might want to skip the cocktails for a bit. There are a few resources that may be within reach: If you have a Sonic Drive-In nearby, they sell 10-pound bags of pebble ice as part of their regular menu. Some gas station mini-markets will also let you buy a plastic bag full of their "crunch ice" (same thing). Barring those venues, breaking up some ice cubes by placing them in the palm of your hand and cracking them hard with the back of a barspoon is a bit of a tedious, but effective, substitute. A mallet & Lewis bag (or rolling pin & Ziploc bag) will pulverize your ice, but is a little harder to control size consistency.

 Slush Ice will be the result of blending, starting with cracked ice cubes or pebble ice.

If **Cloudy Ice** is all you have to work with, it's not the end of the world. Just understand the issues with cloudy ice: trapped air & particulates make it melt faster and shatter more easily. You won't get slow, gentle dilution, so you have to work around it. As a substitute for rock ice or ice cubes in a glass, pre-chill the glass and pack it as full as you can with ice to create a unified thermal mass that will slow down dilution a bit. For stirring, pack a chilled mixing glass two-thirds full of ice and stir as directed in the Techniques section, keeping an extra-careful eye on how much dilution is happening. When shaking, pre-chill your mixing tins and only fill the shaker about one-third full at the most and shake for the absolute shortest amount of time you can, then double-strain to catch ice shards that have exploded into your drink. An open box of baking soda in your freezer can help capture some off-smells that may infiltrate your ice.

SPIRITS form the cornerstone of your home bar supplies. The brands I recommend are based on my years of tasting and testing (you're welcome). When stored properly, spirits can last indefinitely, so you can take your time exploring. I've made an effort to keep things realistic and accessible (for The Basics in particular), but there are some items that will require an effort to locate. Product availability may vary in your region and regulations governing the online purchase and shipping of alcohol differ from state to state, country to country. A quick style note regarding the terms "proof" versus "ABV" — outside the US, the term ABV (alcohol by volume) is the standard. The US term "proof" simply describes a number that's double the ABV. Both terms are required on US liquor labels, so in the interest of better international communication, I'll go with ABV. Where I discuss "overproof" spirits, I'm referring to anything bottled at greater than 50% ABV. You'll notice mentions of the two basic kinds of stills that are used

for making spirits: pot stills and column stills. **Pot stills** evolved from the early alembic stills, and they're known for retaining a wide range of the compounds that create flavor and aroma. One hindrance of pot stills is they can only handle one batch at a time, from start to finish. With an eye on efficiency, Irishman Aeneas Coffey invented **column stills** in the early 1800s to enable continuous, large-scale distillation through multiple passes.

Column stills create a more pure spirit at a higher ABV than what can be achieved through a pot still — but also softer flavors. Sometimes that's the goal. It's a trade-off.

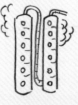

Whiskey is a catch-all term describing spirits made with any type of grain, (generally) distilled to less than 95% ABV, and aged in oak. Production of **bourbon whiskey** has strict rules in place — it must be produced in the United States, made from a mash bill of at least 51% corn, distilled to no more than 80% ABV, and aged at no more than 62.5% ABV in new, charred oak barrels. Besides corn, typical components of its mash bill may include malted barley, rye, and wheat. *{Recommended bourbons: Buffalo Trace, Wild Turkey, Four Roses Single Barrel, Weller 12 Year, Blanton's}* Bonded or "Bottled in Bond" bourbon has an additional set of regulations: it must be the product of a single distillation period, made by one distiller at one distillery (not blended), aged in a federally-supervised ("bonded") warehouse for at least four years, and bottled at 50% ABV. You'll find use for both standard-strength and **overproof bourbon** whiskey; it's good to keep something in the 40% - 45% range in stock as well as the more fiery (and flavorful) 50% - 65% style. *{Recommended overproof bourbons: Old Grand-Dad Bonded, Wild Turkey 101}* Traditionally, bourbon has a Southern upbringing (Bourbon County, Kentucky specifically), but it's currently made across the US.

Rye whiskey originated in New England and is likewise made across the country. It's become a bartender's darling over the last 15 years for its spicy, assertive character. Rye's specifications mirror those of bourbon with one exception: its mash bill must be at least 51% rye. A bottle of **overproof rye** is a must. *{Recommended ryes: Pikesville, Russell's Reserve, Wild Turkey, George Dickel} {Recommended overproof ryes: Rittenhouse Bottled In Bond, Wild Turkey 101}* **Tennessee whiskey** is similar to bourbon, but differs in two distinctive ways: at the start of fermentation, a bit of mash from a previous batch is added to kickstart the process (like using a sourdough starter), and then between the still and the barrel, the spirit undergoes slow filtration through sugar-maple charcoal to remove impurities (known as the "Lincoln County Process"). *{Recommended Tennessee whiskies: Uncle Nearest, George Dickel, Nelson's Green Brier}* The most renowned style of **malt whiskey** is **Scotch whisky**, and it's in a class of its own: revered and somewhat reluctant to be mixed. Note they spell it without the 'e' — as do **Japanese whisky** producers who originally emulated the Scotch style but now are respected as vanguards in their own right. Malt whiskey must be at least 51% malted barley. Malting is a process where cereal grain is moistened and allowed to begin germinating, then that process is halted by drying. Malting converts the grain's starches to sugars, and also breaks down proteins so they can be fermented by yeast. "Single malt whisky" doesn't mean it's made from a single kind of malt, but rather it's made at a single distillery using a pot still. Blended Scotch whisky employs both malt whisky and grain whisky (made from grains other than barley, typically corn, rye, or wheat). Aging typically occurs in oak barrels previously used for bourbon. A minimum of three years is required, and for sipping, 18 years seems to be the sweet spot. Older doesn't necessarily mean better: Don't fall into the trap of thinking a 24-year-old Scotch is better than a 12-year-old Scotch by default. Sometimes too much barrel is... too much. Broad and diverse, Scotch whisky styles range across the country in five geographic regions with distinct styles: Lowlands (soft and floral), Speyside (complex, fruity, and spicy), Highlands (full of terroir with heather, oak, and peat), Campbeltown (fruit and maritime brine), and the flavor-bombs of Islay (wild and aggressive peat smoke). In the rare cocktail where they play well with others, a blended Scotch or a Highlands style is preferred. You'll also want an Islay whisky to use as an accent occasionally. *{Recommended Scotch whiskies: The Famous Grouse, The Macallan, Glenmorangie} {Recommended Islay Scotch whiskies: Ardbeg, Laphroaig} {Recommended Japanese whiskies: Nikka, Toki, Hibiki, The Yamazaki}* In the decades bookending 1900, **Irish whiskey** was the go-to for bartenders due to its affability in mixing and pronounced green-apple fruitiness. To keep up with demand, there were hundreds of distilleries and over 400 brands produced in Ireland. Then came Prohibition, two World Wars, the Irish Civil War, and the Great Depression... leaving Ireland with only two operating distilleries. Thankfully, a resurgence of this once-endangered spirit is in bloom — over the last 10 years, the number of distilleries has increased from three to 18. *{Recommended Irish whiskies: Jameson, Redbreast 12, Tullamore D.E.W.}* **Canadian whisky** has been overlooked in the current cocktail renaissance, but keep your eyes peeled for stereotype-busting, high-quality products. *{Recommended Canadian whiskies: Lot 40, Forty Creek}*

Genever, referred to as "Holland gin" in old cocktail books, is the Dutch predecessor of British gin. Made in Holland of distilled maltwine (a blend of corn, rye, wheat, and other grains), genever was originally made as a medicinal drink of crushed juniper berries distilled with brandy. As wine grapes became scarce, malty beer mash was substituted to keep the product rolling — and to great effect. In this way, genever is kind of a weird cousin to both whiskey and gin — similar to both, but tasting like neither. *{Recommended genever: Bols}*

Gin, in case you didn't know, is just flavored vodka. Perhaps the only kind of flavored vodka I can endorse, at that. It begins with a blank-canvas spirit at 96% ABV (all the better to extract essential flavor compounds), typically made of grain, but not always. This spirit is then re-distilled or infused with a potpourri that may include roots, fruits, herbs, and spices in custom blends of these botanicals. Primary among these (particularly for the London Dry style) are Italian juniper berries, the source of most of gin's distinctive piney, herbal note. England embraced gin in the 1680s, when the Dutchman William of Orange assumed the English throne and desired a locally-produced version of the Dutch genever. By 1810, the lightly-sweetened **Old Tom gin** style came into play: drier than genever, with the emphasis on other botanicals besides juniper. Worth tracking down if you're curious about historical accuracy are barrel-aged Old Toms. *{Recommended Old Tom gins: Hayman's, Ransom, Citadelle}* **Plymouth gin** is both a style and a singular brand. It's been produced at the Black Friars Distillery since 1793 (at least) and is notable for its dryness, earthy minerality, and boosted botanicals — with juniper taking a less-dominant position. *{Recommended Plymouth gin: Plymouth}* The **London Dry gin** designation defines its production process: all flavors must be added during distillation using only natural botanicals, and nothing can be added afterward besides water (to bring it to the desired ABV) and a small amount of sugar. This style came into vogue in the 1840s and by 1900 had won the world over. Crisp, juniper-forward and bracing, it makes the Martini. *{Recommended London Dry gins: Beefeater, Fords Gin, Sipsmith, Tanqueray}* The "**New Western**" style of gin bends the "juniper first" rule, playing with other botanicals like hops, grapefruit, and lavender. *{Recommended New Western gins: Aviation, Bimini,*

Future} Occasionally, you'll have a need for a **flavored gin**: look for brands that use natural ingredients. *{Recommended flavored gin: Malfy con Limone}*

 Vodka saw a surge in popularity between the 1940s and the 2000s due to its super-neutral flavor profile and nearly-invisible mixability. It can be made from literally anything containing sugars, but grain and potato vodkas are dominant. It's typically distilled in at least two passes through a column still, and is distilled to at least 96% ABV before water is added to adjust for the desired ABV. Surprisingly, there's a lack of transparency for such a clear spirit — don't fall for fancy bottles or promises of quadruple distillation and diamond filtering — an honest product will deliver value and quality. *{Recommended vodkas: Absolut, Luksosawa, Stolichnaya, Seagram's 100 Proof (for prep recipes)}*

Brandy refers to any spirit distilled from fruit, but grapes are most common. **Cognac** and **Armagnac** are French grape brandies, distilled in traditions reaching back to the 1600s to exacting standards and guidelines that determine everything from its source grapes to the time of year it can be made, to the type of barrels it ages in (Limousin or Tronçais oak). Certain notable **California brandy** producers emulate and expand on the French traditions, employing a wider range of grape varietals and production nuances. Where I call for cognac in a recipe, a high-quality California brandy is an acceptable substitute. *{Recommended cognacs: Courvoisier, Martell, Hine}* *{Recommended California brandies: Germain-Robin, Osocalis, Argonaut}*

American **Apple Brandy** or **applejack** and French **Calvados** are two notable cousins from a similar tree —George Washington is on record as a fan of Laird's in particular. *{Recommended apple brandies: Laird's 86 Applejack, Laird's Bottled in Bond Straight Apple Brandy}* **Peach Brandy** was a thing in Colonial times and is now all-but-impossible to come by... but don't worry, I have a hack in the prep section *(pg 210)*. **Pisco** is a Peruvian and Chilean brandy made of Muscat or Italia grapes, crushed and fermented with their skins, distilled in pot stills, and then rested in glass or stainless steel before bottling. *{Recommended piscos: Caravedo, Barsol}* **Grappa** is a similar unaged grape brandy from Italy, made from a variety of grapes depending on local preference, including

Nobile, Sangiovese, Chianti, Brunello, or
Moscato. {*Recommended grappa: Knight
Gabriello di Nobile, di Chianti, and di
Brunello*}

Mezcal is a fascinating spirit, complex
and delicate in its flavor and its production.
It's made from over 50 varieties of the
succulent agave (not a cactus, not an aloe).
The bulk of agave (or *maguey*, as they also
refer to it) harvested for mezcal grows in
and around the southern Mexican state of
Oaxaca. After harvesting, the agaves are
stripped of their spiky *pencas,* then their
dense, fibrous interior hearts *(piñas)* are
slowly smoke-roasted over days in earthen
pits lined with red-hot river
rocks and local hardwoods
like mesquite or *guamúchil*.
The roasted piñas are then
trimmed of any over-charred
parts, shredded or crushed, and
left to slowly ferment in open-
air vats that become graced
with wild, ambient yeasts.
Distillation occurs in pot
stills — sometimes even clay
pots in the celebrated *minero*
style. By law, mezcal must be
bottled at the distillery where
it's produced, not transported
in bulk for bottling elsewhere.

Agaves take eight to 12 years to mature, so the lead time to create mezcal has tempted some producers to take shortcuts that negatively affect long-term goals related to economic sustainability and environmental impact. Mezcal is a spirit that will benefit from your thoughtfulness as a consumer: Do your own research and learn about the people and practices behind the brands. *{Recommended mezcals: Del Maguey, Montelobos, Ilegal, Don Amado, Alipús, Machetazo}*

Tequila is a sub-category of mezcal,  native to Jalisco, that can only be made from one kind of agave: the Blue Weber. Differing from the broader mezcal style, tequila eschews smoky pit-cooking in favor of roasting in large brick ovens called *hornos*. Tequila was originally imported to the US in the late 19th century as a health tonic, not a beverage alcohol — but it didn't take long for that to change.

Blanco tequila is most common in cocktails. It's typically unaged, but it can be barreled up to just shy of two months. Reposado ("rested") tequilas see time in used bourbon, rye, or brandy oak barrels anywhere from two to 12 months. Añejo ("aged") expressions take on more barrel flavor and softer agave character after one to three years. Rare (and pricey) Extra Añejo varieties can go as long as 21 years under exacting conditions. Look for tequila that declares itself as 100% Blue Agave (to avoid *mixto* products cut with cheaper distillates) and research the use of diffusers in tequila production, another corner-cutting process with significant long-term impacts. *{Recommended tequilas: Cimarrón, Fortaleza, Siete Leguas, Espolón, Tequila Ocho}*

Rum is one of the most challenging spirits to understand and to categorize, primarily because of the vastness of its production area (anywhere tropical, mostly) where local styles and customs have shaped its evolution. The old recipes calling for light, gold, or dark rums may have worked so-so when there were only a handful of available products to choose from, but with the vast range of rums available today, we've learned that a light Jamaican rum and a light Cuban-style rum have about as much in common flavor-wise as a jerk pork sandwich and a sugar cookie. Adding to the fog surrounding rum is its history. Most spirits have unfortunate legacies related to colonialism or slavery, but rum in particular

bears this stain prominently with the common categorizations of British-style, Spanish-style, and French-style. Grouping diverse and distinct individual rums in honor of those who colonized their producing regions no longer seems respectful.

So, even though it's a bit rambling and broad, I'll group rums by their island (or country) of production. Admittedly, flavor profiles and production methods can vary even within these groups, but we gotta do something to get our heads around rum, right? These are broad strokes and I'm only covering areas of production called for in this book's recipes. All the rums detailed here (until we get to rhum agricole) are molasses-based: in an industrial process, sugar cane is boiled and refined to make granulated sugar, and the leftover dark, syrupy byproduct is molasses. **Barbados rum** comes from the birthplace of Caribbean rum (first distilled there in the 1640s). Barbadians prefer a blend of pot-still and column-still rum, with an emphasis on balanced body and elegant barrel nuances. *{Recommended Barbados rums: Mount Gay XO, Doorly's 12, Plantation Barbados 5}* **Jamaican rum** is known for its "hogo" — the funky, musty, pungent character that comes as a result of long fermentation with the wild yeasts and bacteria that inhabit the island plus, in some cases, the use of "dunder" and "muck" (leftover distillation waste, dead yeast cells, scraps of sugar cane, even rotting fruit). Sounds gnarly, tastes amazing. In Jamaican rums, you'll find hogo in widely varying degrees from a subtle perfume to fight-or-flight-inducing. *{Recommended Jamaican rums: Appleton, Hamilton Pot Still Black, Wray & Nephew, Coruba, Smith & Cross Navy Strength}* **Demerara rum** (from Guyana) has a dry, smoky gunpowder essence. The notorious 151 strength is most commonly used as the firecracker ka-pow in classic tropical drinks. *{Recommended Demerara rums: El Dorado 12, Lemon Hart 151, Hamilton 151}* What I refer to broadly as **Cuban-style rum** is produced in a range of places: Cuba of course (although currently legally unavailable to the US due to a long-standing embargo — and I would never recommend finding a way around such a precious and important law), but similar-style rums are also made in Puerto Rico, Nicaragua, Mexico, and Panama. When the Communists under Fidel Castro took over Cuba, they seized Havana Club's production facilities at gunpoint. Members of the Arechebala family (who owned the brand) were either imprisoned or fled for Spain and the United States. Havana Club's later master distiller, Don Pancho, made a run of working under Castro, but eventually relocated to Panama where he continues his craft at his own distillery, Las Cabras. Adding to the chaos, there's currently an ongoing legal dispute between the global liquor giants Pernod Ricard and Bacardi over rights to the name "Havana Club." If you do have access to the real Cuban Havana Club (not the Puerto Rican knockoff version), grab a bottle. Think purity with Cuban-style rum: blanco expressions are notable for their confectionery brightness, typically aged for three years then charcoal-filtered to remove color. Longer-aged expressions are all about simplicity and directness — the cane and the barrel dancing across your palate in enchanting soft spirals. The Black Strap style takes a hard right turn to the gritty side of Molassestown. *{Recommended Cuban-style rums: Havana Club Añejo 3 Años, Matusalem Platino, Matusalem Gran Reserva 15, Panamá-Pacific 9, Cruzan Black Strap}*

Rhum agricole from Martinique, Guadeloupe, Marie-Galante, and Reunion Island employs a different production style from other kinds of rum: rather than starting with molasses, they go straight to the source and crush fresh sugar cane to extract its juice for a quick fermentation. The mash is distilled in specialty "Créole" column stills modified from French stills used for Armagnac. The resulting rum retains all the grassy notes you'd expect from freshly-crushed sugar cane. Aged expressions spend three months to three years in used bourbon barrels. Less commonly, these Caribbean locations also produce a "rhum industriel" made of molasses, not fresh cane. *{Recommended rhums agricole: Rhum J.M, Neisson, Clément, Damoiseau, Duquesne}* **Blended rums** add a whole other set of complications to the mix, but are indispensable for their thoughtful customization to suit specific drinks. *{Recommended blended rums: Plantation 3 Stars, Denizen Merchant's Reserve, Banks 5 Island, Banks 7 Golden Age, Plantation Stiggins' Fancy, Plantation O.F.T.D.}* One more oddball rum is called for: the unexpectedly Austrian, strangely butterscotch, and thoroughly dangerous Stroh 160.

Cachaça is the spirit of Brazil, similar to rhum agricole in its source material of fresh sugarcane. Made since the early 1600s, cachaça (by regulation) may only be distilled once to its final ABV. Most modern cachaças are made in pot stills, retaining all the funky, grassy character of this tropical spirit. *{Recommended cachaças: Novo Fogo, Avuá, Ypióca, Pirassununga 51}*

Nonalcoholic Spirits, essentially distilled water with a blend of distilled natural flavors, are a nascent trend just finding its footing. Inclusion in your home bar can make non-imbibing guests feel equally welcome; they may be worth it just for that. *{Recommended nonalcoholic spirit: Seedlip Spice 94}*

AMARI are traditional European after-dinner *digestivo* sips with a range of health-specific botanicals added, always with a bitter component — usually Gentian. In traditional medicine, the root of the flowering Yellow Gentian was used as an anti-inflammatory stomach tonic both to help stimulate appetite and ease digestion. Now, when you hear "bitter," don't think it's going to be nasty and disgusting. If you like good chocolate or good coffee, your palate already understands how pleasant bitterness can be when combined with sweetness. It's like life, you know — you take the good with the bad. The most common style of amaro production uses a neutral spirit base (typically vodka or grappa) loaded up with botanicals (roots, bark, herbs, flowers, spices), sugar, and, sometimes, caramel coloring. Typical amari botanicals may include anise, chamomile, chinchona, ginger, lemon balm, licorice, mint, orange peel, rhubarb, saffron, sage, thyme — even artichoke at the weird end of things. These are often regional family recipes passed down through generations. Amari can be kept at room temperature (their sugar content helps keep them shelf-stable), and they range in ABV from 20% to 40%, so they can be a great option when you don't want something too strong. *{Recommended amari: **Campari**, Aperol, Fernet-Branca, Branca Menta, CioCiaro, Averna, Ramazzotti, Montenegro, Nonino, Meletti, Sfumato, Cynar, Suze, Gran Clasico, Bigallet China-China}*

BITTERS are legally considered to be "non-potable" (undrinkable), but that hasn't stopped the bold from including them as full-blown recipe components. These intensely-flavored infusions and tinctures with roots in the medicinal tonics of the 18th century have seen a surging revival over the last 20 years, with all manner of esoteric and creative variations. Angostura still reigns as the gold standard, but a few more help enliven cocktails both new and old. *{Recommended bitters: **Angostura Aromatic & Cocoa**, **Miracle Mile Forbidden**, **Miracle Mile Orange** or **Regan's Orange**, **Bitter Truth Creole** or **Peychaud's**, **Bitter Truth Celery**, **Bitter Truth Bogart's**}*

FORTIFIED & AROMATIZED WINES: VERMOUTH & QUINQUINA can be thought of similar to amari — they're just made with a fortified wine base ("fortified" in strength and for longevity with a spirit, usually neutral spirit or grappa). **Vermouth** is aromatized with botanicals including wormwood (from the German *wermut*) as one of the bitter components (where it's allowed). After its early beginnings in China, it came to rise in Germany as a digestive tonic for the upper class, something they would take a sip of between each bite so they could keep gorging themselves, striving for the overweight appearance prized as a status symbol. But German vermouth had a reputation as ruthlessly efficient and equally unpleasant. It took tavern worker Antonio Carpano of Turin, Italy to bring his family's recipe to his bosses in 1786, a finessing of the idea of vermouth for German customers with a blend of sweetness and spice. The French style is referred to as "dry;" the Italian style as "sweet." **Quinquina** are distinguished by the predominance of chinchona bark as their bitter component. Both vermouth and quinquina are great over ice with a lemon or orange twist as a simple aperitif to mark the border between the workday and the evening. Keep aromatized wines stored in the refrigerator after opening, buy small bottles if they're available, and use them before they go stale, typically two weeks. *{Recommended vermouths: Dolin Dry, Rouge, & Blanc, Cocchi Vermouth di Torino, Carpano Antica Formula, Noilly Prat Dry & Rouge, Punt e Mes} {Recommended quinquinas: Cocchi Americano, Lillet Blanc, Kina L'Aero d'Or, Dubonnet, Byrrh}*

FORTIFIED WINES: SHERRY, PORT, & MADEIRA are wine-based products of Spain and Portugal. **Sherry** (from Jerez in Andalusia, on Spain's Mediterranean coast) gets a dose of brandy after fermentation to increase its ABV, then is aged in wood, picking up oxidation and all those barrel notes familiar to whiskey drinkers: caramel, vanilla, and leather. Sherry employs the solera method that blends the contents of older and younger barrels to capture the best of both worlds. Different varieties abound — in this book's recipes, we'll call for fino, Amontillado, Manzanilla, and Pedro Ximénez. **Port**, from northern Portugal's Douro region, is boosted with aguardiente during fermentation to arrest that process and leave residual sugars in place, then typically sees two to six years in wood. The tradition of making **Madeira** off the coast of Spain comes from a happy accident, when barrels of wine had been shipped across the Atlantic, didn't sell, and were returned to Portugal. On its return, the winemakers found that sun exposure and agitation inside the barrel from the long voyage had a positive effect on the wine, so they emulated that effect using heat and aging. The "rainwater" style of Madeira is mostly sold in the US — elsewhere, look for Verdelho Madeira. Keep fortified wines stored in the refrigerator and use them before they go stale, typically two weeks. They're all lovely for sipping neat, chilled, after dinner. *{Recommended fortified wines: Lustau Fino, Amontillado, and Manzanilla Sherry, Hidalgo Pedro Ximénez Sherry, Graham's Fine Ruby and Six Grapes Port, Broadbent Rainwater Madeira}*

LIQUEURS are spirit-based, typically flavored with fruits, nuts, herbs, or flowers, and are heavy on sugar for stability, texture, and flavor. Some have a fabled history (like Chartreuse from 1605), others are more recently available (like Ancho Reyes from 2013). Note that "crème de" liqueurs don't contain cream — they're so-named for their creamy texture. Liqueurs (with the exception of Pimm's and Bailey's, which require refrigeration) will keep for years at room temperature and away from direct sunlight. {*Recommended liqueurs: Ancho Reyes, Bailey's Irish Cream, Becherovka, Bénédictine, B.G. Reynolds or homemade falernum, Briottet crème de abricot, crème de mûre, and crème de peche, Chambord, Chartreuse (green and yellow), Cherry Heering, Clément Créole Shrubb, Cointreau, Frangelico, Gabriel Boudier Crème de Cassis, Galliano, Grand Marnier, Herbsaint, J.M Shrubb, Luxardo Sangue Morlacco Cherry, homemade nocino, Koloa Kaua'i Coffee, Lazzaroni Amaretto, Licor 43, Maraska maraschino, Meletti, Merlet crème de poire, Pernod absinthe, Pierre Ferrand Dry Curaçao, Pimm's #1, Ricard pastis, Senior curaçao, **St. Elizabeth or homemade pimento dram**, St. George spiced pear liqueur*

*& NOLA coffee liqueur, **Tempus Fugit** crème de cacao, crème de banane, crème de menthe, and crème de noyeaux}*

SUGARS will be used primarily for making syrups, but they do come into play on their own in a few drink recipes. **White sugar** is bright and direct. **Cane sugar** has a bit more body. **Demerara sugar** contains molasses and is essential for depth of flavor in many classic drinks — turbinado is an acceptable substitute. If you can't find **superfine sugar**, or if you are the thrifty type, you can run regular sugar through your blender or spice grinder to reduce the size of the crystals and *voilà*: superfine sugar! Never use "powdered sugar" in drinkmaking — it contains cornstarch for the purpose of making frosting. If you can, buy locally-made **honey** instead of a grocery-store brand. You'll be getting a better product, and the bees will thank you. *{Recommended sugars: white sugar, cane sugar, demerara sugar, honey}*

SYRUPS & CORDIALS can be made at home — recipes are in the Prep section. **Syrups** are any form of sugar or fruit purée transformed with water so they become more easily mixable than the sugar on its own. They can also deliver a spice element to a cocktail when infused with elements like cinnamon or vanilla, which is sometimes the case with **canne syrup** of the Caribbean. **Cordials** employ fruit juice as the blending agent instead of water or purée. Both cordials and fruit-purée syrups benefit from a dose of overproof spirit to guard against spoilage. All should be refrigerated. *{Recommended syrups: simple syrup, rich simple syrup, rich Demerara syrup, honey syrup, agave nectar, canne syrup, maple syrup, ginger syrup, vanilla syrup, cinnamon syrup, citrus syrup, coconut syrup, passion fruit syrup, homemade fassionola, homemade or Small Hand Foods orgeat, Small Hand Foods tonic syrup and pineapple gum syrup} {Recommended cordials: grenadine, lime cordial, grapefruit cordial}*

LENGTHENERS are those ingredients that bring dilution to Grogs and fizz to Collinses and Punches. Keep a cold iSi soda siphon on standby for **seltzer** or to make quick **sodas** using syrups and juice. To conserve on space and double-dip on the utility of syrups, I prefer to only purchase commercial sodas if there's no easy way to make them fresh at home. Most are fairly straightforward, so it's no big deal to prep a quick ginger soda, for example, as part of the process of making your overall drink. If you choose to purchase ginger soda, select a brand with a prominent, spicy, fresh-ginger flavor. A couple recipes call for **coffee** or espresso — make these with your preferred roast, as fresh as possible, and on the strong side since they'll be added to other ingredients. **Tea** finds its way into more recipes than you might expect. Make it fresh if you can. {*Recommended homemade lengtheners: seltzer, tonic soda, ginger soda, lemon soda, lemon-lime soda, orange soda, grapefruit soda, coffee, espresso, unsweetened black and green tea, unsweetened chai tea*} {*Recommended commercial lengtheners: Mexican Coca-Cola and Squirt, Jarritos Toronja, Fever Tree Tonic Water, Barritt's Ginger Beer, Reed's Extra Ginger Brew, Sanpellegrino Limonata and Aranciata Rosso*}

FRUITS & JUICES require some planning ahead: citrus will only last a few days sitting out at room temperature. I try to keep a couple Eureka **lemons,** Bearss **limes**, and Valencia or Navel **oranges** on hand at all times (for juicing and for garnishes). White "Oro Blanco" **grapefruit** are preferred, but can be difficult to come by; pink grapefruit is acceptable. Never refrigerate citrus —

your refrigerator acts as a dehumdifier that accelerates the drying-out of citrus. Barring the luxurious privilege of growing your own citrus or grabbing some from a neighbor's tree, if you have access to a farmer's market or produce stand, make an effort to buy there instead of at the grocery store. Local, seasonal citrus will invariably be of higher quality than fruit that's been picked too early, super-chilled during shipping, and trucked or flown from elsewhere. Admittedly, the climate where you live may not be suitable for good citrus — just do your best. Look for citrus that feels heavier than it appears, is smoothly rounded (not starting to square off and have its ribs showing through), and has fragrant oil in its rind (press the end of the fruit with your thumb to see and smell the oil). Never settle for bottled, pasteurized lemon, lime, or orange juice — the flavors are off and your drinks won't be near the level you're hoping to achieve. Here and there, you'll need **strawberries**, **raspberries**, and **blackberries**. Fresh is best (it's actually kind of fun to enjoy seasonal foods and drinks, then miss them when they're gone), but in some cases, frozen is acceptable — I'll specify in those recipes if you can get away with frozen. Fresh **pineapple** juice is amazing but a bit of a pain to make: I typically carve and rough-chop pineapple, run it through the blender to purée until smooth, then it has to pass through a sieve to separate any big chunks. Unsweetened 100% pineapple juice in a carton is a reluctantly-acceptable substitute, but definitely avoid canned pineapple juice —there's no getting around that metallic taste. A **cucumber** and a ripe **banana** drop in to a couple of recipes. You'll use bottled **pomegranate** juice to make grenadine. Ensure it's not blended with other juices or sweetened. Bottled **cranberry** juice is used sparingly, but still look for 100% unsweetened juice. You'll also need some frozen 100% **fruit purées** on occasion. *{Recommended citrus and fruit: Valencia or Navel oranges, Eureka lemons, Bearss (aka Persian) limes, Oro Blanco or Pink grapefruit, strawberries, raspberries, pineapple, cucumber, banana} {Recommended juices: POM Wonderful 100% juice, Ocean Spray unsweetened Pure Cranberry} {Recommended frozen purées: passion fruit, guava, white peach}*

MARKET GOODS are common (and occasionally not-so-common) items that find their way into cocktails and preparations: things like **milk** and **heavy cream** (aka whipping cream), **produce**, and some canned or bottled goods. Pre-whipped cream won't work the same as freshly-whipped. If you can, source fresh **eggs** from a local provider or farmer's market. Don't substitute iodized table salt for **kosher salt**. A wide variety of spices come into play in these recipes, but whole **nutmeg**, ground fresh, is essential. Any of the extremely Not-So-Basic items that may be unfamiliar or hard to come by locally will have online options listed in the resources section after the index. I won't list every last little market good here — just refer to the details of each recipe before you dive in to ensure you're ready.

Various ways of making and employing **GARNISHES** will be discussed in the Techniques section next, so in addition to the previously-mentioned fresh mint and citrus you'll have on hand, there's just a couple more things: cherries, green olives, and such. Cocktail cherries don't require refrigeration, but brined garnishes do. {*Recommended garnishes: **Fabbri Amarena cherries**, **pimiento stuffed cocktail olives**, pitted Castelvetrano olives, cocktail onions, cocktail umbrellas, rock candy demitasse sticks, chocolate-covered cherries, beef jerky*}

BEER styles you'll want to keep on hand are driven by your personal preference and that of your guests, perhaps even some seasonal choices. There are three inherent elements in beer that influence their styles: malt, yeast, and hops. Beer styles will typically lean into one of these three elements: classic English-style ales, like **porters**, **stouts**, and **amber ales**, showcase malt with flavors of caramel and toffee; funky **sours** and **farmhouse ales** are all about yeast and can taste of banana, clove, or wet hay; while everyone knows that hops give **pale ales** and **IPAs** their piney intensity. **Lagers** and **pilsners** unite all three of these elements into classic harmonies to create the world's most popular beer styles. With the explosion in craft brewing, it seems almost every area has reasonable access to a great hometown brewery or a bottle shop that curates a local selection — and buying locally is the best advice I can give you. Not only will you be supporting your neighborhood's economy and rewarding the hustle of entrepreneurs, but you'll be enjoying fresher, higher-quality brews and a wider variety of distinct, esoteric styles (sometimes driven by uncommon varieties of hops the big, national brewhouses aren't interested in). Canned beer used to have a stigma, identified exclusively with cheap, watery, mass-market swill, but the truth is, cans keep beer fresher by blocking the sunlight that turns beer skunky — especially true with imported beer that's had more time in transit to degrade. Definitely avoid clear or green bottles. Most big brands have diluted the souls of their brews, but here's the good news: There's a decent number of breweries who started small and stayed true to their roots that now enjoy national distribution. *{Recommended nationally-distributed breweries: Anchor Brewing, Bell's Brewery, Dogfish Head Brewery, Firestone Walker Brewing Company, Sierra Nevada Brewing Company, Stone Brewing}*

CIDER is an emerging player here in the US that never really went away in its homes of England, France, and Spain. Colonists to New England, where grain for beer doesn't grow well, brought Old World cidermaking traditions (and apple tree rootstock) with them. It took westward expansion, a wave of German immigrants to the midwest with their strong preference for beer, and Prohibition to remove cider from our national palate. Growers were left no choice but to chop down heirloom orchards and replace them with crops they could sell — and now the search to recover those lost apple varieties is an ongoing effort. Over the last 15 years, a revival of American cidermaking has found a comfortable middle space between the worlds of beer and wine: joining in the free-form, creative, "hand of the producer" energy of the craft beer scene, while honoring the core traditions of its roots as does winemaking. Jumping on the apple-cart bandwagon, some producers have cut corners by growing miniature trees, rushed to maturity with overwatering, while those playing the long game are content to stick with standard rootstock or semi-dwarf apple varieties that take longer to mature (and offer richer flavors including the deep tannins essential to great cider). As you'd expect, the best American ciders come from places where the best apples are grown: the Pacific Northwest, the Great Lakes, and New England — while the notable Old World cider centers never stopped. Quality imported and domestic brands can be found, but be prepared for a bit of a quest. *{Recommended American cider: ANXO Cidery, Eden Ciders, Eve's Cidery, Fable Farm Fermentory, Finnriver Farm & Cidery, Shacksbury Cider, South Hill Cider, West County Cider}*

{Recommended imported cider: Christian Drouin, Domaine Dupont, Eric Bordelet, Gurutzeta, Oliver's, Peckham's, Sandford Orchards}

The vast world of **WINE** can be categorized in many ways, but I've found a rudimentary, shorthand approach of looking at 11 essential grape varietals to be useful. After all, when we experience wine, we're tasting grapes. **Cabernet Sauvignon** holds the throne as the King of Reds. It's grown around the world, but it finds its highest-quality homes in Napa Valley, California, and Bordeaux, France (where you'll find it labeled as its region, not its varietal — the European way of honoring notable, historic epicenters of winemaking). Cabernet Sauvignon is a big, bold red bursting with black fruits like black currant and blackberry — but also accented with menthol and bay leaf. *{Recommended Cabernet Sauvignon wines: J. Lohr Seven Oaks, Grgich Hills, Regusci, Heitz Cellars}* **Syrah** is another bold, hearty varietal with fruit flavors ranging from black plum to blueberry and savory roasted meats. Great producing regions include the Rhône Valley in France, California's central coast, and Australia (where it wears the original Persian name

"Shiraz"). *{Recommended Syrah wines: Qupé, Guigal, Maison Chapoutier, Delas Frères}* **Pinot Noir** is lighter-bodied, delicate, and more approachable, with tart red fruit notes like cherry and strawberry, pleasantly grounded with mushroomy earthiness. It's what the French label as "Burgundy," after its growing region in France. California does well with this grape in Santa Barbara, the Sonoma Valley, and Sonoma Coast; it's also excellent in Oregon's Willamette Valley, New Zealand, and Australia. *{Recommended Pinot Noir wines: Talbott Kali Hart, Patz & Hart, Kosta Browne}* **Sangiovese**, from Italy's Tuscany region, is the source of the magical, food-friendly Chianti. This wine ranges from medium- to full-bodied and revels in flavors of stewed red fruits, sun-dried tomato, and Mediterranean herbs. *{Recommended Sangiovese wines: any straw-covered bottle of Chianti (have fun), Marchesi Antinori Badia a Passignano}* Spanish **Tempranillo** makes Rioja, a favorite wine for Sangria due to its easy-drinking, medium body character. *{Recommended Tempranillo wines: Kirkland Rioja, La Rioja Alta}* Misunderstood and maligned **Merlot**, a cousin of King Cab, is soft and plush at its best, with flavors of black fruit and briny black olives... but most bottles are just average. Look for offerings from Pomerol, Bourdeaux, for its finest expression. *{Recommended Merlot wines: Raymond, Château Lafleur-Gazin}* A similar reputation unfortunately saddles the Queen of Whites, **Chardonnay**. When it's great, it's great: Burgundy, France, does it right, with luscious apple, pear, pineapple, and mango notes. Their Chablis style bypasses the usual oak aging for a direct experience of the grape. California's central coast versions lean tropical in their flavors, while Sonoma and Napa can be more crisp. At its least interesting, Chardonnays can be flabby, oaky, butter-bombs with zero acidity — but the ones that aren't are worth the search. *{Recommended Chardonnay wines: Au Bon Climat, Ramey, Morlet Family Vineyards}* **Sauvignon Blanc** makes a crisp, super-tart wine that tastes of peaches and tropical fruits. New Zealand and Napa Valley, California, make exceptional versions. France has two options: the Loire Valley calls it "Sancerre," after its region,

and also makes it as "White Bordeaux." *{Recommended Sauvignon Blanc wines: Brander, Cloudy Bay, La Doucette}* The best **Riesling** wines are German in origin. They can be lemon-lime tart, but are balanced with honeyed apricot sweetness in varying degrees. *{Recommended Riesling wines: Loosen Bros. Dr. L, Fritz Haag}* Good old **Pinot Grigio** is softer than Sauvignon Blanc, crisp with bitter lemon, grassy and floral. Best found from Italy and France (as Pinot Gris). *{Recommended Pinot Grigio wines: anything from the Friuli region, Trimbach, Schlumberger}* Spanish and Portugeuse **Albariño** is tart and fresh, full of Valencia orange blossom and peel. *{Recommended Albariño wines: Luzada Rias Baixa, Paco & Lola}* Austrian **Grüner Veltliner** is light in body, lemony, and grassy, even veering into piney hops. *{Recommended Grüner Veltliner wines: Stadlmann, Domane Wachau Federspiel Terrassen}* **Rosé** is not a grape varietal, but a style of making wine in which red grape skins are allowed to ferment along with their juicy, white interiors for a

period, then removed. Versions from Provence, France, are unparalleled. *{Recommended rosé wines: St Supéry, Bonny Doon Vin Gris de Cigare}* Sparkling wines like **Champagne** and **Prosecco**, typically made of Pinot Noir and Chardonnay grapes, are wonderful for special occasions (and also find their way into a few cocktails as lengtheners). The dry French "Brut" style is  the gold standard emulated by California producers in Mendocino and Sonoma. *{Recommended sparkling wines: Krug Grande Cuvée Brut, Moët & Chandon Imperial, Bianca Vigna, Mionetto, SR262}* Treat wine carefully — don't keep it in a hot car while running errands, store in a cool, dark place. Reds can benefit from a quick 10-minute refrigeration, but keep whites and sparkling wines cold, removing them 10 minutes before serving. The funny practice of smelling the cork before you taste a wine is actually useful. If you give the side of the cork a sniff (not the end) and detect an odor of musty, moldy, wet cardboard, you have a wine that's been "corked" — negatively affected by TCA, a chemical compound left over from sterilizing wood. The effect can be subtle or dramatic, a little off or undrinkable. Go ahead, sniff that cork!

TECHNIQUES

A shorthand legend leads off each recipe, specifying the **method** for making that drink, its serving **glass**, and what type of **ice** (if any) will be in the finished drink.

method	glass	serving ice (if any)
SHAKE	**ROCKS**	**CUBES**

You'll stir a Manhattan identically as you stir a Martini. Build an Old Fashioned and a Negroni the same. Equal shakes applies to a Margarita and a Daiquiri. No need to repeat the details of these methods for every recipe — once you get them down, you'll know what I mean when I say "build" or "dump." Occasionally, there will be oddballs that require some special instructions — for those, I'll break it down directly in the recipe. But the vast majority will adhere to one of the following methods.

BUILD & STIR

This method assembles the finished drink right in the glass. Dilution in built drinks evolves, becoming a journey: the first boozy sip gradually softens to a

whisper as you enjoy it.

1 Prepare the garnish and set it aside.

2 If the recipe calls for expressed citrus oil, squeeze a twist to express oil directly into the glass. Reserve the twist for garnishing, if specified.

3 Add ingredients to the glass, then carefully lower the ice in, using a barspoon for support if needed.

4 With the barspoon, stir the drink for 20 to 30 seconds, with the back of the barspoon in contact with the interior wall of the glass. Ensure any dense ingredients on the bottom are well integrated.

5 Give the citrus twist a final spritz over the surface of the drink and then (if specified as a garnish) slip into the glass, hugging the interior wall. Otherwise, garnish as specified.

SWIZZLE

Swizzled drinks are also built directly in the glass (typically a tall one), but they receive an additional super-chilly treatment of quickly agitating the ice. By lowering the temperature of the drink and the glassware together, continued dilution happens more slowly.

1 Prepare the garnish and set it aside.

❷ Add any non-spirit ingredients to the glass. Add ice to the glass, then slowly pour the spirit over the ice.

❸ Insert a barspoon or swizzle stick directly down the center of the glass to the bottom. Holding it between your palms, quickly rub back and forth (like you're trying to start a fire using a stick) to spin the barspoon or swizzle stick for five seconds.

❹ Work the bottom of the barspoon or swizzle stick up and down in the glass vertically to further mix the drink.

❺ Garnish as specified.

STIR & STRAIN

Stirred drinks are served without ice and consumed relatively quickly, before they get warm. Dilution and chilling here happens entirely outside the serving glass.

❶ Chill your serving glass in the freezer at least 30 minutes. If possible, keep a few coupes and a couple of small rocks glasses for Sazeracs in a safe spot in the freezer at all times to avoid delays.

❷ Gather all your required ingredients, tools, and prepared garnishes to minimize the amount of time from preparation to serving.

3 Add your drink ingredients to the mixing glass.

4 Add ice cubes to your mixing glass, filling it about three-quarters full. You'll want ice stacked above the surface level of the liquid. Holding the barspoon like a pencil pointing straight down, stir smoothly for 20 to 30 seconds, minimizing the amount of agitation. The bowl of the spoon should ride the interior wall of the mixing glass while you stir clockwise with your index finger pushing down from noon to six, then your middle finger pushing up from six to noon. The goal is to create a silky texture, avoid making bubbles, and stir just enough to chill and dilute. You'll see the liquid level rising in the mixing glass as ice melts into your drink, and the exterior of the mixing glass should feel cold to the back of your fingers.

5 Using a Julep or Hawthorne strainer, pour the drink into the chilled glass. Spoon out any stray ice chips that found their way in.

6 If called for, express citrus oil over the surface of the drink and garnish with the twist, or garnish as specified.

SHAKE

Shaking a drink adds
dilution, drops the drink
temperature a bit below
stirring, and creates

an aerated texture. A general rule of
thumb if unsure: drinks containing
citrus, cream, or egg get shaken. These
instructions assume you're using a two-
piece mixing tin set — if not, just follow
along and add ice to your shaker last.

1. Prepare the garnish and set it aside.
2. Measure all ingredients into the
   smaller "cheater" tin. If the recipe
   calls for egg, crack the egg into a
   separate container first to inspect for
   any bits of eggshell.
3. Add ice cubes to the Boston tin,
   about half full. Secure the two tins
   together snugly (the cheater tin will
   fit inside the Boston tin at a slight
   angle) and raise them to shoulder
   level, oriented horizontally, with
   the base of the cheater tin pointed
   behind you.
4. Shake briskly for 10 seconds, then
   separate the tins by squeezing or
   smacking the Boston tin at the point
   where the two meet. The mixed
   drink and ice should all be in the
   Boston tin side of things.
5. Add any lengtheners called for to the

tin (like seltzer or soda), then strain into your glass, using a Hawthorne strainer (or double strain by pairing with a fine-mesh strainer, if the drink contains anything chunky).

6 Garnish as specified.

WHIP

Similar to shaking, but uses a scattering of pebble ice instead of ice cubes and a quicker, faster shake. These instructions assume you're using a two-part mixing tin set — if not, just follow along and add ice to your shaker last.

1 Prepare the garnish and set it aside.

2 Measure all ingredients into the smaller "cheater" tin.

3 Add a small handful of pebble ice to the Boston tin. Secure the two tins together snugly (the cheater tin will fit at a slight angle) and raise the tins to shoulder level, oriented horizontally, with the base of the cheater tin pointed behind you.

4 Shake hard for five seconds, then separate the tins by squeezing or smacking the Boston tin at the point where the two meet. Return any portion of the cocktail residing in the cheater tin to the Boston tin.

5 Pour the drink, including any

remaining bits of ice, over fresh ice in your glass.

❻ Garnish as specified.

DUMP

"Dumping" a drink is almost the same as shaking, but skips the final step of straining out the ice. This method of preparation typically uses pebble or cracked ice.

❶ Prepare the garnish and set it aside.

❷ Measure all ingredients into the smaller "cheater" tin.

❸ Add ice to the Boston tin, approximating just under the volume of your serving glass. Secure the two tins together snugly (the cheater tin will fit at a slight angle) and raise the tins to shoulder level, oriented horizontally, with the base of the cheater tin pointed behind you.

❹ Shake briskly for 10 seconds, then separate the tins by squeezing or smacking the Boston tin at the point where the two meet. Return any portion of the cocktail residing in the cheater tin to the Boston tin.

❺ Pour the drink, ice and all, into the glass.

❻ Garnish as specified.

ROLL

Rolling a drink protects its texture against foaming and is gentler than shaking. You'll only use this for a Bloody Mary (or Red Snapper or Bloody Maria), but it's worth it to keep the ingredients from "breaking." Rolling requires a two-part mixing tin set — although you could use two pint glasses or Mason jars in a pinch.

1. Prepare the garnish and set it aside.
2. Measure all ingredients into the smaller "cheater" tin.
3. Add ice cubes to the cheater tin, about half full. Rest the two tins together, with the lip of one just resting on the lip of the other.
4. Gently tip the tin containing the drink to pour it into the other tin. Change the positions of what tin rests in the other and gently pour it back. Repeat back and forth five times.
5. Pour the drink, ice and all, into the glass. Top with additional ice as needed.
6. Garnish as specified.

FLASH BLEND

Flash blending requires — you guessed it — a blender. This method, popularized by the bars Don the Beachcomber and La Floridita in the 1930s, creates a coarse slush texture and quickly chills the drink.

❶ Prepare the garnish and set it aside.

❷ Measure all ingredients into the blender, including the volume of ice specified in the recipe.

❸ Secure the lid and quickly blitz the drink with a few on-and-off pulses for no more than five seconds.

❹ Pour the drink, ice and all, into the glass.

❺ Garnish as specified.

BLEND

The goal of blending is an even, consistent texture and the integration of any bits and chunks into the drink on the whole — sometimes with ice (in the form of a frozen drink) and sometimes without ice (in drinks that are batched, then chilled in the refrigerator).

❶ If specified, prepare the garnish and set it aside.

❷ Measure all ingredients into the

blender, including the volume of ice specified in the recipe, if called for.

❸ Secure the lid and run the blender on its highest setting for a minimum of thirty seconds, but no more than required to homogenize the drink.

❹ Pour the drink, ice and all, into the glass or proceed with the recipe as directed.

❺ Garnish if specified.

NEAT

Couldn't be easier: pour it into a glass. Done.

Fresh citrus **GARNISHES** add flavor and visual appeal. For a **twist**, use a Y-peeler to remove a strip of citrus peel about one inch wide by four inches long. When peeling, grip the citrus firmly and peel at a right angle to the direction of your fingers, ending away from your thumb. Beware: oily citrus and sharp blades aren't a good combo. Press your fingertips into the fruit to get a good

grip and avoid accidents. To express citrus oil into your glass or across the top of your drink, hold the twist gently between the thumb and first two fingers of each hand with the exterior of the rind pointed toward the glass and pinch. Drinks that get a twist garnish always get a spritz of oil on their surface; some get the oil and then the garnish is discarded. More straightforward are a variety of citrus cuts to form a **wedge**, a **wheel**, or a **half-wheel**. For wedges, snip the ends of the citrus and cut into six to eight wedges. Trim out the center membrane and then give the wedge a notch at the center so it can rest on the rim of the glass. Wedges give people the option of adding more acidity to a drink if they choose. Wheels are more decorative than functional — simply cut slices following the line of the fruit's "equator." Half-wheels are those same slices cut in half; both get notched. Remove any large seeds without mangling the garnish too much. Garnishes on picks, like **cherries**, **olives**, and **onions**, may be positioned in the glass or resting across the rim, whatever floats your boat. The "**flag**" garnish captures a citrus half-wheel and a cherry on the same pick. **Mint** should be lightly clapped or squeezed just before adding it as a garnish to release its fragrance. The

banana dolphin on page 152 is a goofy little art project using a banana half, cloves for eyes, and a cherry in its stem-end mouth. Drinks containing egg white should use the freshest, best-quality eggs you have access to: inferior eggs can have a bit of a "wet dog" smell on top (Golden Retriever, to my nose) — a spritz of citrus oil and an **Angostura décor** can help offset that. To make the décor, arrange drops of bitters around the top of the drink, then drag a cocktail pick through them in a circular fashion. For garnished **rims** of sugar, salt, or spice blends, rather than dip the glass down into the material, go around the sides instead. Moisten the edge of the glass and roll it through your material.

Rimming just half the glass allows guests the option of enjoying the drink with or without the rim.

In recipe legends that specify "no ice," have **CHILLED GLASSES** ready: coupes, fizz glasses, and champagne flutes.

OLEOSACCHARUM, a Latin word meaning "oil sugar," is a fragrant and flavorful syrup that's the first step in making punch, lemonade, and citrus sodas. In the appropriate vessel, combine the recipe's specified amounts of citrus peel and sugar, then muddle them (or squeeze and rub together by hand) to slightly abrade the peels and begin expressing their oil into the sugar. Let them hang out together approximately four hours (maybe more, maybe less — it all depends on how oily your citrus is). Stir them occasionally to keep integrating the sugar into the syrup that's evolving. It's done when the sugar is no longer gritty and you have a consistent texture.

STORAGE is the secondmost vexing challenge for home bartenders (after ice). Without knowing your personal abilities or restrictions, I can only offer some general advice: be realistic about what you'll be drinking and only stock the bottles and tools you need. Avoid storing in direct sunlight or near heat — spirits won't go bad, but they will gradually evaporate, and some liqueurs can oxidize.

Now, ready to make some drinks?

The Old Fashioned is essentially the original cocktail. While the practice of mixing various ingredients with beverage alcohol goes back thousands of years, the specific inclusion of bitters is what makes this drink a "cocktail," as far the historical usage of the term goes. To make bitters, dried roots, barks, spices, citrus peel, edible flowers, and other botanicals are given a bath in high-proof spirit to extract their essential compounds, an old folk-medicine practice. The first known bitters were patented in London in 1712 as a cure-all tonic to help settle the stomach or to mix with wine or brandy as a hangover cure. Around 1750, people started adding a bit of sugar and water to their concoctions to make the flavor more palatable. Calling this a mix a "cocktail" first saw print mention in 1806, when it had transitioned from the medicine cabinet to become a recreational delight. As the century marched on, an array of new drinks emerged with unique names, so people then came to specify this one as the "Old-Fashioned Cocktail." The Pendennis Club in Louisville, Kentucky, standardized the name and recipe as a bourbon drink — but perhaps more than any other drink recipe, this one is adaptable to just about any spirit you care to try. During Prohibition's restricted access to "the good stuff" and as palates changed, people started to add muddled oranges, cherries, and other "garbage" to make the drink work for them. A drowning in seltzer was the final disgrace. And that way became the standard until the next turn of the century, when bartenders returned to the original 19th-century formula of spirit, sugar, water (as ice), and bitters — with a little spray of citrus oil that perfectly unifies the caramel and vanilla of the whiskey with the earthy baking spices of the bitters. What's old is new again.

OLD FASHIONED

traditional | 1750s

BUILD & STIR | ROCKS | ROCK ICE

expressed orange and/or lemon oil

3 dashes Angostura bitters

1 tsp rich demerara syrup

2 oz overproof rye or bourbon whiskey

Garnishes: orange twist, lemon twist,
or both — cherry if you feel like it

WISCONSIN OLD FASHIONED

traditional / Wisconsin / 1890s

BUILD & STIR | ROCKS | PEBBLE ICE

Muddle:

2 dashes Angostura bitters

1 orange half-wheel

1 amarena cherry

1 tsp rich simple syrup

Add:

2 oz brandy

1 oz lemon-lime soda

OAXACA OLD FASHIONED

Phil Ward, Death & Co / New York / 2000s

BUILD & STIR | ROCKS | ROCK ICE

expressed orange oil

3 dashes chocolate-chile bitters

1 tsp agave syrup

½ oz mezcal

1 ½ oz reposado tequila

Garnish: orange twist

'TI PUNCH

traditional / Martinique / 1750s

SWIZZLE | ROCKS | PEBBLE ICE

2 tbsp pebble ice

1 lime coin *(express oil and juice)*

1 tsp canne syrup

2 oz Martinician rhum

Garnish: spent lime coin

MINT JULEP

traditional | Colonial America | 1750s

BUILD & STIR | JULEP CUP | PEBBLE ICE

Gently press to coat cup interior:

8 mint leaves

½ oz rich demerara syrup

Add:

2 ½ oz bourbon whiskey

Mound pebble ice to top,

serve with a straw. Garnish: mint sprig

GEORGIA JULEP

traditional | Colonial America | 1750s

BUILD & STIR | JULEP CUP | PEBBLE ICE

Gently press to coat cup interior:

8 mint leaves

½ oz rich demerara syrup

Add:

2 ½ oz peach brandy

Mound pebble ice to top,

serve with a straw. Garnish: mint sprig

ISLAND OLD FASHIONED

Joseph Schwartz, Little Branch

New York | 2000s

BUILD & STIR | ROCKS | ROCK ICE

expressed orange oil

2 dashes Angostura bitters

1 tsp falernum

2 oz aged Jamaican rum

Garnish: orange twist

HOT TODDY

traditional | Scotland | 1650s

BUILD & STIR | GEORGIAN | WARM

1 tsp demerara sugar

2 oz boiling water

Express lemon oil over, stir to
dissolve sugar, then add:

2 oz blended Scotch whisky

Garnish: clove-studded lemon twist

CORN 'N' OIL

traditional | Barbados | 1730s

Murray Stenson, Zig Zag Café | Seattle | 2000s

WHIP | ROCKS | PEBBLE ICE

½ oz falernum

1 ½ oz blackstrap rum

Mound pebble ice on top,
squeeze lime wedge over

Garnish: lime wedge

IMPROVED GENEVER COCKTAIL

New York | 1860s

BUILD & STIR | ROCKS | ICE CUBES

2 dashes Angostura bitters

2 dashes absinthe

1 tsp rich demerara syrup

1 tsp maraschino liqueur

2 oz genever

Express lemon oil over

Garnish: lemon twist

SAZERAC

Sazerac House | New Orleans | 1850s

STIR & STRAIN | ROCKS | NO ICE

Coat glass interior with:

1 tsp Herbsaint

Separately, stir then strain:

3 dashes Peychaud's bitters

1 tsp rich demerara syrup

2 oz rye whiskey

Express lemon oil over, discard

Variations: substitute cognac or Plantation Stiggins' Fancy rum

MONTE CARLO

David Embury | 1940s

BUILD & STIR | ROCKS | ROCK ICE

expressed lemon oil

2 dashes Angostura bitters

½ oz Bénédictine

2 oz bonded rye whiskey

Garnish: lemon twist

TIKI TODDY

Michelle Bearden, 320 Main | Seal Beach | 2010s

BUILD & STIR | GEORGIAN | WARM

½ oz rich demerara syrup

1 tsp falernum

1 tsp pimento dram

2 oz El Dorado 12 rum

2 oz boiling water

Garnish: clove-studded lemon twist

Vermouth arrived in New York City in the 1840s and '50s with a wave of European immigrants, and by the 1870s it was the hot ingredient in cocktails. Taking the idea of the "improved" cocktail (spirit with sugar, bitters, and a touch of something extra — usually maraschino, absinthe, or curaçao), savvy bartenders nixed the sugar and "something extra" in favor of vermouth, the new darling. Vermouth is simply wine that's been fortified (spiked) with grappa or a neutral spirit, sweetened to various extents, and aromatized with a mix of botanical ingredients like wormwood, cinchona, gentian, cinnamon, citrus peel, lavender, saffron, vanilla, or dozens of others. There's your "something extra" in one easy bottle! As the world underwent rapid change around the turn of the 20th century, these pioneering vermouth cocktails evolved to suit changing tastes. As mid-century approached, the Manhattan dodged a bullet somehow and retained its dignity when compared to other more abused recipes (e.g. Old Fashioned & Martini)... although the late 20th century's lack of interest in rye whiskey left bartenders no choice but to make this with the less-effective, softer bourbon. Thankfully, rye has rebounded in a big way and craft bartenders have fallen in love with the Manhattan's template, rising to the challenge of its deceptively simple structure. A properly made Manhattan is truly a thing of beauty, capturing balance, excitement, and depth in four quick sips while priming your appetite for the evening ahead.

MANHATTAN

New York | 1910s

STIR & STRAIN | COUPE | NO ICE

2 dashes Angostura bitters

1 oz sweet vermouth

2 oz overproof rye whiskey

Optional: express orange oil over

Garnish: cherry

PALMETTO

New York | 1910s

STIR & STRAIN | COUPE | NO ICE

2 dashes Angostura bitters

1 oz sweet vermouth

1 oz aged Cuban-style rum

1 oz dark Jamaican rum

Express orange oil over

Garnish: orange twist

UP-TO-DATE

Hugo Ensslin, Wallick Hotel | New York | 1900s

STIR & STRAIN | COUPE | NO ICE

2 dashes Angostura bitters

¼ oz Pierre Ferrand Dry Curaçao

1 ¼ oz Amontillado sherry

1 ¼ oz overproof rye whiskey

Express lemon oil over

Garnish: lemon twist

EL PRESIDENTE

Havana | 1910s

STIR & STRAIN | COUPE | NO ICE

1 tsp grenadine

½ oz Pierre Ferrand Dry Curaçao

¾ oz blanc vermouth

2 oz aged Cuban-style
   or blended rum

Express orange oil over

Garnish: cherry

Recommended:

Denizen Merchant's Reserve, Banks 7

BOBBY BURNS

New York | 1910s

STIR & STRAIN | COUPE | NO ICE

½ oz Bénédictine

¾ oz sweet vermouth

2 oz Highlands Scotch whisky

No garnish

EMERALD

New York | 1910s

STIR & STRAIN | COUPE | NO ICE

2 dashes orange bitters

1 dash Angostura bitters

1 oz sweet vermouth

2 oz Irish whiskey

Express orange oil over

Garnish: orange twist

HANKY PANKY

Ada Coleman, American Bar at The Savoy
London | 1920s

STIR & STRAIN | COUPE | NO ICE

½ tsp Fernet-Branca

1 ½ oz sweet vermouth

1 ½ oz London Dry gin

Express orange oil over

Garnish: orange twist

VIEUX CARRÉ

Walter Bergeron, Hotel Monteleone
New Orleans | 1930s

BUILD & STIR | ROCKS | ICE CUBES

2 dashes Angostura bitters

2 dashes Peychaud's bitters

¼ oz Bénédictine

1 oz sweet vermouth

1 oz rye whiskey

1 oz cognac

Garnish: lemon twist

DE LA LOUISIANE

Restaurant La Louisiane | New Orleans | 1930s

STIR & STRAIN | COUPE | NO ICE

2 dashes Herbsaint

2 dashes Peychaud's bitters

½ oz Bénédictine

½ oz sweet vermouth

1 ½ oz overproof rye whiskey

Garnish: cherry

REMEMBER THE MAINE

Charles H. Baker | 1930s

STIR & STRAIN | COUPE | NO ICE

1 dash Angostura bitters

1 dash absinthe

¼ oz Cherry Heering

¾ oz sweet vermouth

2 oz overproof rye whiskey

Garnish: cherry

ATLAS

Marco's Liquors | Chicago | 1940s

STIR & STRAIN | COUPE | NO ICE

1 dash Angostura bitters

½ oz curaçao

½ oz 151 Demerara rum

1 ½ oz straight apple brandy

Express lemon oil over

Garnish: lemon twist

BYWATER

Chris Hannah, Arnaud's French 75
New Orleans | 2000s

STIR & STRAIN | COUPE | NO ICE

2 dashes Peychaud's bitters
2 dashes orange bitters
¼ oz falernum
½ oz Green Chartreuse
¾ oz Averna
1 ¾ aged Barbados rum

Express orange oil over
Garnish: cherry

LITTLE ITALY

Audrey Saunders, Pegu Club
New York | 2000s

STIR & STRAIN | COUPE | NO ICE

½ oz Cynar
¾ oz sweet vermouth
2 oz rye whiskey
Garnish: cherry

HISTORIC CORE

John Coltharp | Los Angeles | 2000s

STIR & STRAIN | COUPE | NO ICE

1 dash Angostura bitters
¾ oz sweet vermouth
¼ oz green Chartreuse
¾ oz straight apple brandy
1 oz overproof rye whiskey

Express lemon oil over
Garnish: lemon twist

FRANK LLOYD WRIGHT

Bourbon & Branch | San Francisco | 2010s

STIR & STRAIN | COUPE | NO ICE

2 dashes Angostura bitters

1 tsp nocino

1 tsp Islay Scotch whisky

½ oz crème de poire

2 oz bourbon whiskey

Express lemon oil over

No garnish

BROWN BITTER STIRRED

Jason Schiffer, 320 Main | Seal Beach | 2010s

STIR & STRAIN | COUPE | NO ICE

2 dashes Angostura bitters

¼ oz J.M Shrubb

½ oz Cynar

½ oz Carpano Antica vermouth

2 oz Russell's Reserve
      6 yr rye whiskey

Express lemon & orange oil over

Garnish: rock candy demitasse stick

DOLEMITE

Jason Schiffer, 320 Main | Seal Beach | 2010s

STIR & STRAIN | COUPE | NO ICE

½ oz Cynar

½ oz crème de cacao

2 oz Rittenhouse rye whiskey

Garnish: cherry

(or chocolate-covered cherry)

JON HAMM'S BRIEFCASE

Matt Robold, 320 Main | Seal Beach | 2010s

STIR & STRAIN | COUPE | NO ICE

1 dash Angostura bitters

¼ oz falernum

¼ oz Islay Scotch whisky

¾ oz Amaro CioCiaro

1 ½ oz aged Demerara rum

Express orange oil over

Garnish: orange twist

MOXIE BIRD

Anu Apte, Rob Roy | Seattle | 2010s

STIR & STRAIN | COUPE | NO ICE

2 dashes orange bitters

½ oz Lillet Blanc

1 ½ oz bourbon whiskey

Express lemon oil over

Garnish: lemon twist

THE VELVET TOUCH

Dave Castillo, Truss & Twine
Palm Springs | 2010s

STIR & STRAIN | COUPE | NO ICE

¼ oz Pedro Ximénez sherry

¾ oz Amaro Nonino

2 oz rye whiskey

Express orange oil over

Garnish: orange twist

Is there a cocktail more iconic than the Martini? It's become visual shorthand for all beverage alcohol (warning label icons, emoji, public-intoxication street signs). Right place, right time, and right drink: The Martini captured the imagination of emerging sophisticates in big-city America. The Martini Company (later named Martini & Rossi) began importing their Italian sweet vermouth to the US around 1870, with the French dry style making its stateside debut around 1900. Even though more vermouth brands became available in the US over time (Cinzano, Noilly Prat, Dolin), the name "Martini" for this cocktail stuck. So that should give you a hint about the importance of vermouth to this drink... and still, you get Churchill's snarky comment about "glancing in the direction of" his vermouth on the shelf or the practice of simply wetting the ice with a splash of vermouth and then dumping it out before adding gin. As if vermouth was a nasty, offensive substance. As if! You may have friends who say they hate gin, or they hate vermouth... but I'll gently suggest maybe they just haven't tasted the right gin or the right vermouth, treated properly. The Yin to the Manhattan's flavor-bomb Yang, the Martini is supple elegance in liquid form. For a time in the '90s and '00s, the name "Martini" came to denote any cocktail served in a cocktail glass: think Chocotini, Lychee Martini, Appletini, and so on. Thankfully, we've gotten away from that. The venerable Martini deserves a bit more respect.

MARTINI

New York | 1870s – 1910s

STIR & STRAIN | COUPE | NO ICE

2 dashes orange bitters
1 oz dry vermouth
2 oz London Dry or Plymouth gin
Express lemon oil over
Garnish: lemon twist or olives

TURF COCKTAIL

New York | 1900s

STIR & STRAIN | COUPE | NO ICE

2 dashes orange bitters
1 tsp maraschino liqueur
¾ oz dry vermouth
2 oz London Dry gin
Express lemon oil over
Garnish: lemon twist

MARTINEZ

Bohemian Club | San Francisco | 1880s

STIR & STRAIN | COUPE | NO ICE

2 dashes orange bitters
1 tsp maraschino liqueur
1 ½ oz sweet vermouth
1 ½ oz Ransom Old Tom gin
    or genever

Express orange oil over
Garnish: orange twist

GIBSON

San Francisco | 1890s

STIR & STRAIN | COUPE | NO ICE

¾ oz dry vermouth
2 oz London Dry gin

Garnish: cocktail onion

TUXEDO NO.2

New York | 1910s

STIR & STRAIN | COUPE | NO ICE

1 dash absinthe
2 dashes orange bitters
¼ oz maraschino liqueur
¾ oz dry vermouth
2 oz London Dry gin

Express lemon oil over
Garnish: lemon twist & cherry

FAIRBANK

Robert Vermeire | London | 1920s

STIR & STRAIN | COUPE | NO ICE

2 dashes orange bitters

2 dashes crème de noyeaux

1 ½ oz dry vermouth

1 ½ oz London Dry gin

Express orange oil over

Garnish: orange twist

FITTY-FITTY

Audrey Saunders, Pegu Club | New York | 2000s

STIR & STRAIN | COUPE | NO ICE

2 dashes orange bitters

1 ½ oz dry vermouth

1 ½ oz London Dry gin

Express lemon oil over

Garnish: lemon twist

ANODYNE

Wesly Moore | Eagle Rock | 2000s

STIR & STRAIN | COUPE | NO ICE

3 dashes orange bitters

½ oz Punt e Mes

1 oz Lillet Blanc

2 oz London Dry gin

Express orange oil over

Garnish: orange twist

The ultimate aperitivo (before-dinner) cocktail, the Negroni has become ubiquitous and triumphant on the winning side of the love/hate battle. For some, the bitter-orange Campari is — to put it kindly — an acquired taste. But once you do acquire the taste, there's no going back. You'll want a good, sharp, juniper-forward gin like Tanqueray here — one that won't get beaten down by the other two big-flavor bullies in the drink. The drink has an interesting origin story that goes like this: Italian-born Count Camillo Negroni had spent time in America as a bronco-busting cowboy and in London as a dashing bon vivant. On his return to Florence in 1919, he asked the bartender at the Caffè Casoni for a stronger take on the popular Americano cocktail, swapping gin for seltzer. It caught on locally, and eventually his namesake cocktail became a hit internationally. Proponents of this wonderful story have yet to explain why the Negroni didn't appear in any cocktail recipe books or on any menus until the 1950s, though. Go figure! People drink, they tell stories. Anthony Bourdain was on record as a fan; Gaz Regan was famous (infamous?) for his naughty "finger-stirred Negroni" in simpler times. I've called it "the drink for when you don't feel like having a drink." There's something magical about a well-made Negroni: it's like a reset button for your day, signaling the start of a great night when anything is possible.

NEGRONI

Forsco Scarselli, Caffè Casoni | Firenze | 1910s
Unknown origin | Italy | 1950s
BUILD & STIR | ROCKS | ICE CUBES
1 oz sweet vermouth
1 oz Campari
1 oz London Dry gin
Garnish: orange wheel

MILANO-TORINO

Caffè Camparino | Milan | 1860s
BUILD & STIR | ROCKS | ICE CUBES
1 ½ oz sweet vermouth
1 ½ oz Campari
Garnish: orange wheel

BIJOU

New York | 1880s

STIR & STRAIN | COUPE | NO ICE

1 dash orange bitters
1 oz sweet vermouth
1 oz green Chartreuse
1 oz London Dry gin

No garnish

BOULEVARDIER

Erskine Gwynne | Paris | 1920s

STIR & STRAIN | COUPE | NO ICE

1 dash orange bitters
1 oz sweet vermouth
1 oz Campari
1 ½ oz bourbon whiskey

No garnish

DUNHILL

Hatchett's Bar | London | 1920s

STIR & STRAIN | ROCKS | ICE CUBES

Coat glass interior with:
1 tsp absinthe
Stir:
¼ oz curaçao
1 oz Amontillado sherry
1 oz dry vermouth
1 oz London Dry gin

Express lemon oil over
Garnish: lemon twist

WHITE NEGRONI

Wayne Collins, VinExpo | Bordeaux | 2000s

BUILD & STIR | ROCKS | ICE CUBES

1 oz Suze

1 oz Lillet Blanc

1 oz London Dry gin

Express lemon oil over

Garnish: lemon twist

NEGRONI'S LOSS

Jason Schiffer, 320 Main | Seal Beach | 2010s

BUILD & STIR | ROCKS | ICE CUBES

¾ oz Carpano Antica vermouth

¾ oz Gran Clasico

1 oz genever

Express lemon & orange oil over

Garnish: lemon & orange twists

NEGRONI SBAGLIATO

Mirko Stocchetto, Bar Basso | Milan | 1970s

BUILD & STIR

HIGHBALL | ICE CUBES

1 oz Campari

1 oz sweet vermouth

1 oz prosecco

Garnish: orange wheel

CALLOOH CALLAY

Jason Schiffer, 320 Main | Seal Beach | 2010s

STIR & STRAIN | COUPE | NO ICE

1 dash orange bitters
1 oz Amaro Nonino
1 oz manzanilla sherry
1 oz Malfy con Limone gin

Express lemon oil over, garnish: olive

RUSTY NAIL

21 Club | New York | 1960s

BUILD & STIR | ROCKS | ICE CUBES

3 dashes orange bitters
½ oz Drambuie
2 oz blended Scotch whisky

Garnish: lemon twist

GODFATHER

IILVA Saronno | Lombardy | 1970s

BUILD & STIR | ROCKS | ICE CUBES

½ oz amaretto
2 oz blended Scotch whisky

Garnish: lemon twist
Variation: substitute cognac for a
French Connection

CARAJILLO

Mexico | 1930s

BUILD & STIR | ROCKS | ICE CUBES

1 ½ oz Licor 43
1 ½ oz cold espresso

No garnish

CAFFÈ CORRETTO

Italy | 1930s
BUILD & STIR | PUNCH CUP | WARM
1 oz grappa
1 oz espresso
Garnish: lemon twist

BLACK RUSSIAN

Gustave Tops, Hotel Metropole
Brussels | 1940s
BUILD & STIR
ROCKS | ICE CUBES
1 ¼ oz coffee liqueur
¾ oz vodka
No garnish

BRAVE BULL

Industrias Vinicolas Pedro Domecq
Mexico City | 1960s
BUILD & STIR
ROCKS | ICE CUBES
1 ¼ oz coffee liqueur
¾ oz reposado tequila
No garnish

STINGER

Reggie Vanderbilt | New York | 1900s
STIR & STRAIN | COUPE | NO ICE
¾ oz crème de menthe
2 oz cognac
No garnish

SHERRY COBBLER

unknown origin | 1820s

BUILD & STIR

JULEP CUP | PEBBLE ICE

Muddle:

¼ oz rich demerara syrup

2 orange wheels

Add ice and:

3 ½ oz Amontillado sherry

Mound pebble ice to top, serve with a straw

Garnish: lemon wheel, seasonal fruit, mint

BAMBOO

Louis Eppinger | San Francisco | 1880s

Chris Day | Oakland | 2010s

STIR & STRAIN | COUPE | NO ICE

1 dash orange bitters

1 dash celery bitters

1 ½ oz dry vermouth

1 ½ oz fino or manzanilla sherry

Express lemon oil over

Garnish: lemon twist & olive

ADONIS

Joe McKone, Hoffman House | New York | 1880s

STIR & STRAIN | COUPE | NO ICE

2 dashes Angostura bitters

1 ½ oz Italian vermouth

1 ½ oz Amontillado sherry

Express lemon oil over

Garnish: lemon twist

CHRYSANTHEMUM

New York | 1910s

STIR & STRAIN | COUPE | NO ICE

3 dashes absinthe

1 oz Bénédictine

2 oz dry vermouth

Express orange oil over

Garnish: orange twist

KIR ROYALE

Canon Félix Kir | Dijon, Burgundy | 1940s

BUILD & STIR | FIZZ | NO ICE

Ensure glass & all ingredients
are chilled first.

½ oz crème de cassis

5 oz brut Champagne

Express lemon oil over

Garnish: lemon twist

BELLINI

Giuseppe Cipriani, Harry's Bar | Venice | 1930s

BUILD & STIR | FIZZ | NO ICE

Ensure glass & all ingredients
are chilled first.

1 oz white peach purée

5 oz prosecco

No garnish

CHAMPAGNE COCKTAIL

London | 1860s

BUILD & STIR | FLUTE | NO ICE

Ensure glass & all ingredients are chilled.

Douse to combine:

1 demerara sugar cube

4 dashes Angostura bitters

*Add the soaked sugar cube
to the glass, then add:*

³⁄₄ oz cognac

5 oz brut Champagne

*Express orange and
lemon oil over*

No garnish

MULLED WINE

traditional | Italy | 100s

BUILD & STIR | PUNCH CUP | WARM

*In a crockpot or nonreactive saucepan over
low heat, combine and heat gently:*

2 cinnamon sticks

5 whole cloves

5 crushed cardamom pods

1 tsp chopped ginger

½ tsp grated nutmeg

zest of one orange

½ cup demerara sugar

¼ cup cognac

1 750 mL bottle Beaujolais wine

SERVES 5

Sours

The Daiquiri was standardized by Jennings Cox, an American mining engineer working in Santiago, Cuba around 1896. But mixing rum with citrus and sugar was nothing new to the Caribbean, nor to Colonial Americans who hovered around the communal punch bowl, nor to British sailors who were issued daily rations of rum, limes, sugar, and water as "grog" as far back as 1740. But where those naval grogs were primarily thin via dilution with ample water, the sour style went straight to the point with a little single-serving flavor bomb. In its beginning, a Sour was any spirit with lemon and sugar — and not overwhelmingly tart, as the name might suggest. Cocktail historian David Wondrich has uncovered an 1856 menu from Mart Ackermann's Saloon in Toronto, Canada, that lists a Gin Sour and a Brandy Sour. In his pioneering 1862 book, How to Mix Drinks, or the Bon Vivant's Companion, Jerry Thomas includes the Gin Sour and Brandy Sour as members of a family of drinks, along with their antecedents: punches, crustas, and daisies. A recipe for a Rum Sour appears in the 1895 cocktail book The Mixicologist. Shaking the old rum, lime, and sugar formula with ice may have been the official crowning of the Daiquiri as we know it, sometime in the late 19th century. Eventually, the drink fell into popular misuse as an overly-sweet frozen slushy and shorthand (at least in New Orleans) for a stomach-churning array of unrelated frozen drinks with grain alcohol and artificial flavors. Cocktail enthusiasts *have come to appreciate it as a bit of a "secret shopper" test that determines a bartender's skills and knowledge. When it's done properly, with fresh limes and their fragrant oil, there's simply nothing like a Daiquiri.*

DAIQUIRI

Santiago | 1890s

SHAKE | COUPE | NO ICE

¾ oz simple syrup

1 oz lime juice

2 oz light Cuban-style or blended rum

Garnish: lime wheel

Recommended spirits: Havana Club 3, Banks 5 Island, Plantation 3 Stars, Plantation Stiggins' Fancy

CAIPIRINHA

traditional | Brazil | 1800s

BUILD | ROCKS | ICE CUBES

Muddle until no longer gritty:

1 lime, cut into eight pieces

1 tbsp white sugar

Add ice and:

2 oz cachaça

No garnish

GIMLET

London | 1870s

SHAKE | COUPE | NO ICE

½ oz lime juice

1 oz lime cordial

2 oz Plymouth gin

Garnish: lime wedge

SOUTHSIDE

Southside Sportsmen's Club | New York | 1870s

SHAKE | COUPE | NO ICE

8 mint leaves

¾ oz simple syrup

¾ oz lime juice

2 oz London Dry gin

Double-strain

Garnish: clapped mint leaf

PISCO PUNCH

Duncan Nicol, Bank Exchange
San Francisco | 1890s
SHAKE | COUPE | NO ICE
3/4 oz pineapple gum syrup
3/4 oz lemon juice
1/2 oz Rioja wine
2 oz pisco
Garnish: lemon twist

WARD EIGHT

Locke-Ober Café | Boston | 1890s
SHAKE | COUPE | NO ICE
1/2 oz grenadine
1/2 oz orange juice
1/2 oz lemon juice
2 oz rye whiskey
Express lemon oil over
Garnish: lemon twist

HOTEL NACIONAL SPECIAL

Hotel Nacional de Cuba | Havana | 1900s
SHAKE | COUPE | NO ICE
1/4 oz rich simple syrup
1/2 oz lime juice
3/4 oz pineapple juice
1/4 oz crème de abricot
1 1/2 oz aged Cuban-style rum
Garnish: lime wheel

WILD-EYED ROSE

Hugo Ensslin, Wallick Hotel | New York | 1900s

SHAKE | COUPE | NO ICE

¾ oz grenadine

1 oz lime juice

2 oz Irish whiskey

Garnish: lime & cherry flag

JACK ROSE

Frank J. May | New Jersey | 1900s

SHAKE | COUPE | NO ICE

¾ oz grenadine

1 oz lime juice

2 oz applejack

Garnish: lime wheel

Variation: 50/50 blend

cognac & straight apple brandy

LA FLORIDA

"Constante" Vert, El Floridita | Havana | 1900s

SHAKE | COUPE | NO ICE

1 tsp curaçao

1 tsp grenadine

1 oz lime juice

¼ oz crème de cacao

½ oz sweet vermouth

2 oz light Cuban-style rum

Garnish: lime wheel

PEGU CLUB

Pegu Club | Myanmar | 1920s

SHAKE | COUPE | NO ICE

1 dash Angostura bitters

1 dash orange bitters

¾ oz lime juice

¾ oz curaçao

2 oz London Dry gin

Garnish: lime zest

SIDECAR

Ritz Bar | Paris | 1920s

SHAKE | COUPE | NO ICE

1 tsp rich simple syrup

¾ oz lemon juice

1 oz Cointreau

2 oz cognac

Express orange oil over

Garnish: orange twist,

optional sugared rim

CORPSE REVIVER NO. 2

Ritz Bar | Paris | 1920s

SHAKE | COUPE | NO ICE

¾ oz lemon juice

¾ oz quinquina

¾ oz Cointreau

¾ oz London Dry gin

Garnish: cherry,

absinthe mist

CHAMPS-ÉLYSÉES

Savoy Hotel | London | 1920s

SHAKE | COUPE | NO ICE

1 dash Angostura bitters

½ oz simple syrup

1 oz lemon juice

½ oz Green Chartreuse

2 oz cognac

Express lemon oil over

Garnish: lemon twist

ROYAL BERMUDA YACHT CLUB

Royal Bermuda Yacht Club | Hamilton | 1930s

SHAKE | COUPE | NO ICE

¾ oz lime juice

¼ oz curaçao

½ oz falernum

2 oz aged Demerara rum

Garnish: lime wheel

TWENTIETH CENTURY

Café Royal | London | 1930s

SHAKE | COUPE | NO ICE

2 dashes orange bitters

¾ oz lemon juice

½ oz crème de cacao

¾ oz quinquina

1 ½ oz London Dry gin

Express lemon oil over

Garnish: lemon twist

CAMERON'S KICK

Harry Craddock, Savoy Hotel | London | 1930s

SHAKE | COUPE | NO ICE

3/4 oz orgeat

3/4 oz lemon juice

1 oz Scotch whisky

1 oz Irish whiskey

Garnish: lemon twist

Variation: substitute 1 1/2 oz blanco tequila & 1/2 oz mezcal in place of the whiskies for a **Charo's Kick**

BROWN DERBY

Vendôme Club | Hollywood | 1930s

SHAKE | COUPE | NO ICE

1/2 oz honey syrup

1 oz grapefruit juice

2 oz bourbon whiskey

Express grapefruit oil over

Garnish: grapefruit twist

ARMY & NAVY

New York | 1940s

SHAKE | COUPE | NO ICE

2 dashes Angostura bitters

3/4 oz orgeat

3/4 oz lemon juice

2 oz London Dry gin

Garnish: nutmeg

LAST WORD

Detroit Athletic Club / 1950s

SHAKE | COUPE | NO ICE

¾ oz lime juice

¾ oz maraschino liqueur

¾ oz Green Chartreuse

¾ oz London Dry gin

No garnish

RANGOON GIMLET

Tony Ramos, China Trader / Burbank / 1960s

SHAKE | COUPE | NO ICE

2 dashes Angostura bitters

½ oz lime juice

1 oz lime cordial

2 oz Plymouth gin

Garnish: mint sprig

CLOISTER

Playboy Bartender's Guide / 1970s

SHAKE | COUPE | NO ICE

½ oz simple syrup

½ oz grapefruit juice

½ oz lemon juice

½ oz Yellow Chartreuse

1 ½ oz London Dry gin

Express grapefruit oil over

Garnish: grapefruit twist

TRINIDAD SOUR

Giuseppe Gonzalez, Clover Club
New York | 2000s

SHAKE | COUPE | NO ICE

1 oz orgeat
¾ oz lemon juice
½ oz rye whiskey
1 ½ oz Angostura bitters
No garnish

RUM CRAWL

Bourbon & Branch | San Francisco | 2010s

SHAKE | COUPE | NO ICE

2 dashes Angostura bitters
¼ oz ginger syrup
¾ oz lime juice
½ oz falernum
2 oz aged Jamaican rum
Express orange oil over
Garnish: orange twist

ANTIQUE LEMON DROP

Jason Schiffer, 320 Main | Seal Beach | 2010s

SHAKE | COUPE | NO ICE

½ oz simple syrup
1 oz lemon juice
¼ oz maraschino liqueur
2 oz genever
Express lemon oil over
Garnish: lemon twist, absinthe mist

LEMON DROP

Henry Africa's | San Francisco | 1970s

SHAKE | COUPE | NO ICE

1 oz simple syrup

1 oz lemon juice

½ oz Cointreau

1 ½ oz vodka

Express lemon oil over

Garnish: sugared rim,

lemon twist

COSMOPOLITAN

Toby Cecchini, The Odeon | New York | 1980s

SHAKE | COUPE | NO ICE

½ oz unsweetened cranberry juice

1 oz lime juice

1 oz Cointreau

1 oz Absolut Citron vodka

Express lemon oil over

Garnish: lemon twist

JASMINE

Paul Harrington, Townhouse
Emeryville | 1990s

SHAKE | COUPE | NO ICE

¾ oz lemon juice

¼ oz Cointreau

¼ oz Campari

1 ½ oz London Dry gin

Express lemon oil over

Garnish: lemon twist

FITZGERALD

Dale DeGroff, Rainbow Room | New York | 1990s

SHAKE | COUPE | NO ICE

2 dashes Angostura bitters

¾ oz simple syrup

1 oz lemon juice

2 oz London Dry gin

Garnish: lemon wheel

PAPER PLANE

Sam Ross, Milk & Honey | New York | 2000s

SHAKE | COUPE | NO ICE

¾ oz lemon juice

¾ oz Aperol

¾ oz Amaro Nonino

¾ oz bourbon whiskey

No garnish

BEEHIVE

Brandon Bramhall, Attaboy | New York | 2010s

SHAKE | COUPE | NO ICE

¾ oz honey syrup

¾ oz lime juice

½ oz Fernet-Branca

1 ½ oz aged Jamaican rum

No garnish

Many have claimed parental rights to the Margarita, but surprisingly, the cocktail most likely originated in London, of all places — as the "Picador" cocktail. In a Sour, the use of a liqueur (Cointreau in the Picador's case) in place of simple syrup bumps the Sour into "Daisy" status and — funny coincidence — "margarita" is Spanish for "daisy." The Margarita stood its ground for almost forty years until it succumbed to the dreaded sour mix slushy style of the '70s, along with the Daiquiri. Tequila itself likewise suffered during that time — its dramatic rise in popularity, coupled with the long lead time for agave to mature and natural variations in agave availability due to weather trends led to a decline in tequila quality as producers cut corners by mixing in different agave varietals, blending tequila with cheap aguardiente (cane spirit) as the "mixto" style, and adding caramel color to suggest an aged "gold" spirit. Redemption began to arise in the early '70s with the designation of Jalisco as an AOC (Appelation of Origin), then in the '80s with the emergence of premium 100% Weber blue agave tequilas, and in the '90s with the creation of the Consejo Regulador del Tequila, the governing body that ensures tequila's integrity. We can thank Julio Bermejo of Tommy's Mexican Restaurant in San Francisco for reinventing the Margarita in a way that gets back to basics and honors the spirit: nix the Cointreau, skip the salted rim, and enjoy el puro sabor del agave. The Tommy's Margarita has become the contemporary craft standard.

TOMMY'S MARGARITA

Julio Bermejo, Tommy's Mexican Restaurant
San Francisco | 1980s

DUMP | ROCKS | ICE CUBES

½ oz agave nectar
1 oz lime juice
2 oz blanco tequila
Garnish: lime wheel

MARGARITA

Café Royal | London | 1930s (as "Picador")

SHAKE | COUPE | NO ICE

1 tsp rich simple syrup
1 oz lime juice
1 oz Cointreau
2 oz blanco tequila
Garnish: salted rim, lime wheel

BARBACOA

Julian Cox, Rivera | Los Angeles | 2000s

SHAKE | DOUBLE ROCKS | ICE CUBES

Muddle:

3 lime wedges

3 medium pieces red bell pepper

1 small piece Fresno chile

Add ice and:

½ oz ginger syrup

¾ oz agave nectar

½ oz lemon juice

2 oz mezcal

Double strain

Garnish: beef jerky

TAKE ME AWAY

Cari Hah, Big Bar | Los Angeles | 2010s

SHAKE | COUPE | NO ICE

Muddle:

3 fresh strawberries, hulled

Add ice and:

¼ oz orgeat

½ oz lime juice

½ oz Green Chartreuse

½ oz Aperol

1 ¼ oz mezcal

Double strain

*Garnish: sugared rim,
sugar-dipped strawberry*

EL GUAPO

Sam Ross, Little Branch | New York | 2000s

BUILD | ROCKS | PEBBLE ICE

Muddle:

4 dashes Cholula red hot sauce

¾ oz simple syrup

½ lime, cut into six pieces

Add ice and:

2 oz blanco tequila

Garnish: salt & pepper rim

REVERSE MARGARITA

Rhum Clément | Martinique | 2010s

SHAKE | ROCKS | ICE CUBES

¾ oz lime juice

¾ oz reposado tequila

1 ½ oz J.M Shrubb

Garnish: lime wedge

SANTA ANA FRUIT CART

Gilbert Marquez | Anaheim | 2010s

SHAKE | COUPE | NO ICE

2 slices fresh cucumber

½ oz simple syrup

½ oz lime juice

1 oz pineapple juice

2 oz mezcal

Double strain

*Garnish: Tajin rim,
cucumber wheel*

WHISKEY SOUR

traditional / 1850s

SHAKE | ROCKS | ICE CUBES

¾ oz simple syrup

¾ oz lemon juice

2 oz bourbon whiskey

Garnish: lemon wheel

WHISKEY SMASH

traditional / 1860s

Dale DeGroff, Rainbow Room / New York / 1990s

BUILD | ROCKS | PEBBLE ICE

Gently press:

4 mint leaves

½ lemon, cut into six pieces

¾ oz simple syrup

Add ice and:

2 oz bourbon whiskey

*Stir to combine, pushing the
lemon pieces and mint to the bottom*

Garnish: mint sprig

> ***Egg whites*** *in a cocktail might sound
> a little freaky at first, but it won't
> take more than a sip to change minds.
> Egg whites contribute a silky, thick
> foam to the top of a drink and become
> a finger-dipping dessert at the end…
> but be aware of the faint "wet dog
> smell." A quick spritz of citrus oil and
> a touch of bitters will handle that.*

BOSTON SOUR

unknown origin | 1880s

SHAKE | COUPE | NO ICE

Briefly dry shake, then shake again with ice:

1 egg white

¾ oz simple syrup

¾ oz lemon juice

2 oz bourbon whiskey

Express lemon oil over

Garnish: Angostura bitters décor & cherry

Variation: Float ¼ oz red wine and skip the

Angostura garnish for a **New York Sour***.*

PISCO SOUR

traditional / Peru / 1900s

SHAKE | COUPE | NO ICE

Briefly dry shake, then shake again with ice:

1 egg white

½ oz simple syrup

¾ oz lemon juice

2 oz pisco

Express lemon oil over

Garnish: Angostura décor

CLOVER CLUB

Clover Club / Philadelphia / 1910s

SHAKE | COUPE | NO ICE

Briefly dry shake, then shake again with ice:

1 egg white

6 raspberries

½ oz simple syrup

½ oz lemon juice

½ oz dry vermouth

1 ½ oz Plymouth gin

Double strain

Express lemon oil over, garnish: raspberry

BUMBLE BEE

Charles H. Baker | 1930s

SHAKE | COUPE | NO ICE

Briefly dry shake, then shake again with ice:

1 egg white

1 oz honey syrup

¾ oz lime juice

2 oz aged Jamaican rum

Express orange oil over

Garnish: orange twist & Angostura décor

WHITE LADY

Harry McElhone. Harry's NY Bar | Paris | 1920s

SHAKE | COUPE | NO ICE

Briefly dry shake, then shake again with ice:

1 egg white

1 tsp rich simple syrup

¾ oz Cointreau

¾ oz lemon juice

2 oz London Dry gin

Express lemon oil over

Garnish: Angostura décor & cherry

AMARETTO SOUR

Unknown origin / 1970s
Jeffrey Morgenthaler, Clyde Common
Portland / 2010s
SHAKE | ROCKS | ICE CUBES
Briefly dry shake, then shake again with ice:
1 egg white
1 tsp rich simple syrup
1 oz lemon juice
¾ oz bonded bourbon whiskey
1 ½ oz amaretto
Express lemon oil over
Garnish: lemon twist & cherry

GOLD RUSH

T.J. Siegel, Milk & Honey / New York / 2000s
SHAKE | ROCKS | ICE CUBES
¾ oz honey syrup
¾ oz lemon juice
2 oz bourbon whiskey
Garnish: lemon wheel

PENICILLIN

Sam Ross, Milk & Honey / New York / 2000s
SHAKE | ROCKS | ICE CUBES
scant ½ oz ginger syrup
scant ½ oz honey syrup
¾ oz lemon juice
2 oz blended Scotch whisky
Float
¼ oz Islay Scotch whisky
Garnish: candied ginger

SCUTTLEBUTT

Jason Schiffer, 320 Main | Seal Beach | 2010s

SHAKE | ROCKS | ICE CUBES

¼ oz simple syrup

1 oz lemon juice

½ oz Licor 43

¾ oz Gran Clasico

¾ oz George Dickel rye whiskey

Express grapefruit oil over

Garnish: grapefruit twist

BRAMBLE

Dick Bradsell, Fred's Club | London | 1980s

SHAKE | ROCKS | PEBBLE ICE

½ oz simple syrup

1 oz lemon juice

½ oz crème de mûre

2 oz London Dry gin

Garnish: blackberries

BOURBON RENEWAL

Jeffrey Morgenthaler, Clyde Common
Portland | 2000s

SHAKE | ROCKS | PEBBLE ICE

1 dash Angostura bitters

½ oz simple syrup

1 oz lemon juice

½ oz crème de cassis

2 oz bourbon whiskey

Garnish: lemon wedge

*The Collins, as a style, is essentially a sour served tall with a little dilution by way of seltzer. Take away the ice and now you're looking at a fizz. Add a spice element, lengthen the dilution, and you'd have a punch. Sours are modular in this way. The history of the Tom Collins is a little hard to pin down — there are stories of a bar prank ("hey, Tom Collins was just in here talking shit about you — he just left for the bar up the street"), hazy evidence linking it to a bartender named Collins... but the obvious answer to at least part of the name is its use of Old Tom gin. Old Tom was **the** gin style in the 19th century, coming into being after the Dutch spirit genever (commonly referred to as "Holland gin" in old recipe books, but not really a gin) and before the London Dry style that took hold around 1900. It's a lightly-sweetened gin with less emphasis on juniper than London Dry, more emphasis on the other botanicals — citrusy and floral. Recently-revived modern interpretations of Old Tom gin skew closer to the London Dry style than may be historically accurate. If you're curious, try a barrel-aged version like Ransom Old Tom for a glimpse of what the original may have tasted like. The Tom Collins is fantastic on a warm afternoon, but I've also found that with the addition of strawberries, it also makes an embarrassingly fantastic frozen drink — see page 153 for the recipe.*

TOM COLLINS

London | 1870s

SHAKE | COLLINS | ICE CUBES

¾ oz simple syrup

1 oz lemon juice

2 oz Old Tom gin

Shake, then add:

1 oz seltzer

Garnish: orange & cherry flag

JOHN COLLINS

Stephen Price, Garrick Club | London | 1830s

SHAKE | COLLINS | ICE CUBES

¾ oz simple syrup

1 oz lemon juice

2 oz genever

Shake, then add:

1 oz seltzer

Garnish: lemon twist

FRENCH 75

London | 1870s

SHAKE | COLLINS | ICE CUBES

¾ oz simple syrup

¾ oz lemon juice

1 ½ oz London Dry gin

Shake, then add:

2 oz brut Champagne

Garnish: lemon twist

Variation: substitute cognac for gin

PLANTER'S PUNCH

traditional | Caribbean | 1700s

SHAKE | COLLINS | PEBBLE ICE

2 dashes Angostura bitters

¾ oz simple syrup

1 oz lime juice

2 oz dark Jamaican rum

Shake, then add:

1 ½ oz seltzer

Garnish: lime wheel

MOJITO

traditional / Caribbean / 1580s (as "El Draque")

WHIP | COLLINS | PEBBLE ICE

8 mint leaves

¾ oz simple syrup

¾ oz lime juice

2 oz light Cuban-style rum

*Top with additional pebble ice,
pushing mint to the bottom of
the glass*

Garnish: lime wheel, mint sprig

QUEEN'S PARK SWIZZLE

Queen's Park Hotel / Trinidad / 1920

WHIP | COLLINS | PEBBLE ICE

8 mint leaves

¾ oz simple syrup

¾ oz lime juice

2 oz El Dorado 3 rum

*Top with additional pebble ice,
pushing mint to the bottom of
the glass, then top with:*

3 dashes Peychaud's bitters

Garnish: mint sprig

SINGAPORE SLING

Ngiam Tong Boon, Raffles Hotel
Singapore | 1900s
Jason Schiffer, 320 Main | Seal Beach | 2010s

SHAKE | COLLINS | PEBBLE ICE

4 dashes Angostura bitters
¼ oz pineapple juice
1 oz lemon juice
1 oz Luxardo cherry liqueur
1 oz Bénédictine
1 oz London Dry gin

Shake, then add:

1 oz seltzer

Garnish: pineapple & cherry flag,
cocktail umbrella

FLORODORA

The Waldorf-Astoria | New York | 1900s

SHAKE | COLLINS | ICE CUBES

Muddle:

4 raspberries
½ oz simple syrup

Add, then shake:

¾ oz lime juice
1 ½ oz London Dry gin

Add:

2 oz ginger soda

Garnish: orange, lime,
and cherry flag

GIN-GIN MULE

Audrey Saunders, Beacon
New York City | 1990s
SWIZZLE | COLLINS | PEBBLE ICE
Gently press:
8 mint leaves
1 oz simple syrup
¾ oz lime juice
Add:

1 ½ oz London Dry gin
1 oz ginger soda
Swizzle
Garnish: mint sprig

KENTUCKY BUCK

Erick Castro, Bourbon & Branch
San Francisco | 2000s
SHAKE | COLLINS | PEBBLE ICE
Muddle:
1 chopped strawberry
¾ oz ginger syrup
Add, then shake:
2 dashes Angostura bitters
¾ oz lemon juice
2 oz bourbon whiskey
Add:

2 oz seltzer
Double strain
Garnish: sliced strawberry

BECHER COLLINS

Jason Schiffer, 320 Main | Seal Beach | 2010s

SHAKE | COLLINS | PEBBLE ICE

Muddle:

2 orange wedges

Add, then shake:

¾ oz simple syrup

1 oz lemon juice

1 oz overproof rye whiskey

1 oz Becherovka

Add:

2 oz seltzer

Garnish: orange wedge

CHARTREUSE SWIZZLE

Marcovaldo Dionysus | San Francisco | 2010s

SWIZZLE | COLLINS | PEBBLE ICE

¾ oz lime juice

1 oz pineapple juice

½ oz falernum

1 ¼ oz green Chartreuse

Garnish: mint sprig, nutmeg

HARDLY WALLBANGER

Eric Johnson, Sycamore Den | San Diego | 2010s

SHAKE | COLLINS | PEBBLE ICE

½ oz vanilla syrup

½ oz lemon juice

2 oz orange juice

1 oz Galliano

1 ½ oz vodka

Add:

2 oz seltzer

Garnish: orange & cherry flag

DETROITER

Jason Schiffer, 320 Main | Seal Beach | 2010s

SHAKE | ROCKS | ICE CUBES

Dry shake briefly to drive off some carbonation, then add ice and shake again:

¾ oz honey syrup

¾ oz lemon juice

¾ oz apple brandy

1 oz Cynar

1 oz India pale ale

Add ice cubes to the glass and:

1 oz India pale ale

Express grapefruit oil over

Garnish: grapefruit twist

You really can't improve on perfection, but that hasn't stopped the world from screwing up Trader Vic's original 1944 Mai Tai for over 75 years. The secretive and combative world of mid-century tropical drinks contributed to its own degradation, as bartenders sought to mimic best-sellers through hit-or-miss reverse engineering,... but Trader Vic himself also changed his recipe as time went on, adding more citrus juices (and more rum). He originally used Wray & Nephew 17-year old Jamaican rum in his recipe, but the drink became so popular he actually depleted the world supply of that rum (or they just stopped making it), then he did the same with the later 15-year expression. These days, many passionate bartenders go with Denizen Merchant's Reserve, a brilliant blended rum made specifically to emulate the rum combo used by Trader Vic in the '50s, or experiment with their own blend of rums. The original Mai Tai will take you back to the flourishing years of the tropical drinks trend, when US military men and women were returning home from World War II's battles in the Pacific Theater, torn between remembering and forgetting what they'd been through over there. They found refuge in this wildly creative — but also appropriated, conflated, and unfortunately racist — fantasy world where Caribbean-style drinks, Cantonese-American food, and Polynesian art were jumbled in an "exotic" mishmash of othering. But damn, those drinks!

MAI TAI

Trader Vic's | Emeryville | 1940s

DUMP | DOUBLE ROCKS | PEBBLE ICE

½ oz curaçao

½ oz orgeat

1 oz lime juice

2 oz Denizen Merchant's Reserve rum

Garnish: spent lime half, mint sprig

Alternate rum blend:

50/50 aged Jamaican rum

& aged Martinician rhum

ZOMBIE

Don the Beachcomber | Hollywood | 1930s

FLASH BLEND | CHIMNEY | PEBBLE ICE

1 dash absinthe

1 dash Angostura bitters

¼ oz cinnamon syrup

¼ oz grenadine

¾ oz lime juice

½ oz grapefruit juice

½ oz falernum

1 ½ oz aged Cuban-style rum

1 ½ oz dark Jamaican rum

1 oz 151 Demerara rum

1 cup pebble ice

Garnish: mint sprig

COBRA'S FANG

Don the Beachcomber | Hollywood | 1930s

FLASH BLEND | COLLINS | PEBBLE ICE

1 dash absinthe

1 dash Angostura bitters

½ oz fassionola

½ oz lime juice

½ oz orange juice

¼ oz falernum

1 ½ oz 151 Demerara rum

1 cup pebble ice

Garnish: cinnamon stick

NUI NUI

Don the Beachcomber | Hollywood | 1930s
FLASH BLEND | COLLINS | PEBBLE ICE
1 dash Angostura bitters
scant 1 tsp vanilla syrup
¾ oz cinnamon syrup
¾ oz lime juice
¾ oz orange juice
scant 1 tsp pimento dram
2 ½ oz aged Cuban-style rum
1 cup pebble ice
Express orange oil over
Garnish: long orange twist

TEST PILOT

Don the Beachcomber | Hollywood | 1940s
FLASH BLEND | DOUBLE ROCKS | PEBBLE ICE
1 dash absinthe
1 dash Angostura bitters
½ oz lime juice
½ oz falernum
½ oz Cointreau
¾ oz light Cuban-style rum
1 ½ oz dark Jamaican rum
1 cup pebble ice
Garnish: cherry

HURRICANE

Louis Culligan, Pat O'Brien's
New Orleans | 1930s
DUMP | SNIFTER | PEBBLE ICE
1 oz fassionola
1 oz lime juice
1 oz dark Jamaican rum
1 oz 151 Demerara rum
Garnish: orange & cherry flag,
windblown cocktail umbrella

EL DIABLO

Trader Vic's | Emeryville | 1940s
DUMP | COLLINS | PEBBLE ICE
¾ oz lime juice
¾ oz crème de cassis
1 ½ oz blanco tequila
Shake, then add
2 oz ginger soda
Garnish: lime wheel

151 SWIZZLE

Don the Beachcomber | Hollywood | 1940s
FLASH BLEND | COLLINS | PEBBLE ICE
1 dash absinthe
1 dash Angostura bitters
½ oz simple syrup
½ oz lime juice
1 ½ oz 151 Demerara rum
1 cup pebble ice
Garnish: nutmeg, cinnamon stick

MISSIONARY'S DOWNFALL

Don the Beachcomber | Hollywood | 1940s

BLEND | SNIFTER | PEBBLE ICE

½ cup mint leaves (packed)

¾ oz honey syrup

¾ oz lime juice

1 oz pineapple juice

½ oz crème de peche

1 ½ oz light Cuban-style rum

1 cup pebble ice

Garnish: pineapple wedge, mint sprig

THREE DOTS AND A DASH

Don the Beachcomber | Hollywood | 1940s

FLASH BLEND | COLLINS | PEBBLE ICE

1 dash Angostura bitters

½ oz honey syrup

½ oz lime juice

½ oz orange juice

¼ oz falernum

¼ oz pimento dram

1 ½ oz aged rhum agricole

½ oz aged Cuban-style rum

Garnish: three cherries & a pineapple wedge

DR. FUNK

Don the Beachcomber | Palm Springs | 1950s

DUMP | COLLINS | PEBBLE ICE

1 tsp absinthe

½ oz grenadine

¾ oz lime juice

1 ½ oz Banks 5 rum
      or light Cuban-style rum

Shake, then add:

1 oz seltzer

Garnish: lime wheel, mint sprig

WESTERN SOUR

Kon-Tiki | various locations | 1950s

DUMP | DOUBLE ROCKS | PEBBLE ICE

¼ oz simple syrup

¾ oz lime juice

¾ oz grapefruit juice

½ oz falernum

2 oz George Dickel rye whiskey

Garnish: pineapple flag, umbrella

JUNGLE BIRD

Hilton Aviary Bar | Kuala Lumpur | 1970s

Giuseppe González, Painkiller | New York | 2010s

DUMP | DOUBLE ROCKS | PEBBLE ICE

½ oz simple syrup

½ oz lime juice

1 ½ oz pineapple juice

¾ oz Campari

1 ½ oz Cruzan Black Strap rum

Garnish: orange wheel

LAPU LAPU

Royal Hawaiian | Laguna Beach | 1960s
Jason Schiffer, Tradecraft Hospitality | 2010s

DUMP | SNIFTER | PEBBLE ICE

¼ oz rich demerara syrup
½ oz passion fruit syrup
1 oz orange juice
1 oz lemon juice
¾ oz Plantation OFTD rum
¾ oz aged rhum agricole

Float:
¾ oz 151 Demerara rum

Garnish: orange & cherry flag, mint sprig

PUKA PUNCH

Ray Buhen, Tiki Ti | Los Angeles | 1960s

FLASH BLEND | CHIMNEY
PEBBLE ICE

1 dash Angostura bitters
¾ oz honey syrup
¾ oz passion fruit syrup
¾ oz orange juice
¾ oz pineapple juice
1 oz lime juice
¼ oz falernum
¾ oz dark Jamaican rum
1 oz aged Cuban-style rum
1 oz light Cuban-style rum
1 cup pebble ice

Float:
¾ oz 151 Demerara rum

Garnish: pineapple, orange & cherry flag

Tropical drinks become high-style in the 1950s, flourishing with the ornate, over-the-top enthusiasm typical of the post-war era. But as the younger generation came to see the effects of the Vietnam War in real time via gutsy reporting on TV, they also began to understand the toxic side of this fantasy world in the context of the civil rights movement and the damage done to others (and ourselves) by American imperialism. The Mai Tais that Dad drank with his square friends were no longer cool. By the '70s, what passed for tropical drinks were sugary crowd-pleasers devoid of nuance, like the Piña Colada (but delicious when made right, see page 177). Unexpectedly, it took the SoCal punk scene of the '80s and '90s to resurrect the abandoned, uncool genre of what they started calling "tiki" — furthering its mishmash by adding rockabilly, hot rods, lounge style, and burlesque into the mix. Among those leading the revival was Jeff "Beachbum" Berry, who began appreciating, researching, and unearthing the lost recipes and ingredients of the original drinks by interviewing aging bartenders and their children… eventually striking gold by unraveling the mystery of Don the Beachcomber's previously unknown 1934 Zombie recipe, among others. The 21st-century craft cocktail movement has come to acknowledge and start to move beyond tiki's problematic past while embracing these astounding drinks for their compatible craft elements: quality spirits, fresh juices, and handmade syrups — but also as a fun antidote to the stiffness and orthodoxy that came with the cocktail renaissance. I'll wrap up this section on tropical drinks with Beachbum Berry's original Ancient Mariner, his superior riff on Trader Vic's Navy Grog. I consider it a "Basic" simply because I wouldn't want to live in a world without this flavor!

ANCIENT MARINER

Jeff "Beachbum" Berry | 1990s

DUMP | DOUBLE ROCKS | PEBBLE ICE

½ oz simple syrup

½ oz grapefruit juice

¾ oz lime juice

¼ oz pimento dram

1 oz El Dorado 12 rum

1 oz Smith & Cross rum

Garnish: lime wedge, mint sprig

RAMOS GIN FIZZ

Henrico Charles Ramos, Imperial Cabinet
Saloon / New Orleans / 1880s

SHAKE | FIZZ | NO ICE

3 drops orange flower water

¾ oz simple syrup

½ oz lemon juice

½ oz lime juice

1 ½ oz Old Tom gin

½ oz heavy cream

Dry shake, then add:

1 egg white

Dry shake again, then add one ice cube and
shake until the ice dissolves, then strain into
the glass and add to the empty shaker:

2 oz seltzer

Swirl to combine with residue, then gently
pour into the glass in a steady stream to lift
the foamy head to the rim of the glass.

Top with:

3 drops orange flower water

No garnish

PEACH BLOW FIZZ

Philadelphia | 1900s

SHAKE | FIZZ | NO ICE

¾ oz simple syrup

1 fresh peach, skinned and cubed

¼ oz lime juice

½ oz lemon juice

2 oz Old Tom gin

Dry shake hard to break down peach, double-strain, return to a clean shaker, then add:

½ oz heavy cream

Add one ice cube and shake until the ice dissolves, then strain into the glass and add to the empty shaker:

2 oz seltzer

Swirl to combine with residue, then gently pour into the glass in a steady stream to lift the foamy head to the rim of the glass.

Top with:

3 drops orange flower water

No garnish

The idea for punch came to British and Dutch sailors by way of India — and from there to the Caribbean and Colonial America. This lineage is evident in the word itself: "punch" comes from the Hindi "panch," meaning "five." Why five? There's a Barbadian rhyme that spells it out: "one of sour, two of sweet, three of strong, four of weak, and a touch of spice to make it nice." Cute, but it would actually make an unbalanced recipe. The goal with punch is balance across all five elements, including dilution by way of water or tea. Boozier versions may use fortified wine or champagne as a lengthener. Punch held dominance in Colonial America's taverns until the mid-1800s, when the pace of life began to quicken and people just couldn't afford to spend hours hanging out and imbibing socially. I can't imagine what they would think of today's instant-gratification world. The decidedly old-school bowl of punch is one of the simplest ways to make sure a large party is sufficiently quenched. Sure, it's a bit of work upfront that you'll need to plan far ahead for, but it frees you — the host — to kick back a bit when your guests arrive. They'll serve themselves and gather around the punch bowl just like in olden days. Plus, punch also has a built-in safety factor: as the bowl depletes, it becomes more diluted, helping ensure guests don't overserve themselves.

WEST INDIES PUNCH

traditional | 1760s

BUILD | PUNCH BOWL | BLOCK ICE

In the bowl, create an oleosaccharum (pg 74):

Peels of 4 lemons and 6 limes

1 cup superfine cane sugar

Add the following, then remove citrus peels:

1 cup lemon juice

1 cup lime juice

4 cups dark Jamaican rum

6 cups cold unsweetened black tea

Garnish: clove-studded lemon slices

and freshly-grated nutmeg

SERVES 20

PHILADELPHIA FISH HOUSE PUNCH

State in Schuylkill / Philadelphia / 1730s

BUILD | PUNCH BOWL | BLOCK ICE

In the bowl, create an oleosaccharum (pg 74):

Peels of 6 lemons

1 cup superfine cane sugar

Add the following, then remove lemon peels:

1 cup lemon juice

½ cup peach brandy

2 cups cognac

1 cup Smith & Cross rum

3 cups aged Jamaican rum

4 cups cold unsweetened black tea

Garnish: freshly-grated nutmeg, lemon wheels

SERVES 20

QUOIT CLUB PUNCH

Richmond / 1780s

BUILD | PUNCH BOWL | BLOCK ICE

In the bowl, create an oleosaccharum (pg 74):

Peels of 6 lemons

1 cup superfine cane sugar

Add the following, then remove lemon peels:

1 ½ cups lemon juice

½ cup Rainwater madeira

1 cup Smith & Cross rum

1 750 mL bottle cognac

Garnish: freshly-grated nutmeg

SERVES 20

HOLIDAY PUNCH

Dave Stolte | 2010s

BUILD | PUNCH BOWL | BLOCK ICE

In the bowl, create an oleosaccharum (pg 74):

Peels of 3 lemons and 3 oranges

2/3 cup superfine white sugar

Add the following, then remove citrus peels:

6 dashes Angostura bitters

2 cups lemon juice

2 cups orange juice

1 cup curaçao

2 cups cognac

2 cups aged Jamaican rum

2 cups cold unsweetened chai tea

Garnish: clove-studded orange wheels, nutmeg

SERVES 20

FRISKY PUNCH

Dave Stolte | 2010s

BUILD | PUNCH BOWL | BLOCK ICE

In the bowl, create an oleosaccharum (pg 74):

Peels of 6 lemons

2/3 cup superfine white sugar

Add the following, then remove lemon peels:

10 dashes Angostura bitters

1 cup grenadine

2 cups lemon juice

4 cups bourbon whiskey

1 1/2 cups cold water

1 1/2 cups brut Champagne

Garnish: freshly-grated nutmeg

SERVES 20

SANGRIA

traditional / Spain / 1490s

BUILD | WINE GLASS | ICE CUBES

1 tsp Angostura bitters
1 oz rich simple syrup
1 cup orange juice
¾ cup curaçao
1 750 mL bottle Rioja wine
Garnish: seasonal fruit

SERVES 5

GARIBALDI

Traditional / Italy / 1830s
Naren Young, Dante / New York / 2010s

BUILD | HIGHBALL | ICE CUBES

In a blender, blend until frothy:
4 oz orange juice
Pour over ice, then add & stir:
1 ½ oz Campari
Garnish: orange wedge

MICHELADA

Michel Esper Jorge / San Luis Potosí / 1970s
Erick Castro / San Diego / 2010s

BUILD | PILSNER | ICE CUBES

1 tsp Tapatio
½ oz simple syrup
¾ oz orange juice
¾ oz lime juice
8 oz lager
Garnish: Tajin rim, lime wedge

BLOODY MARY

"Pete" Petiot, Harry's NY Bar | Paris | 1930s
King Cole Bar | New York | 1940s
ROLL | COLLINS | ICE CUBES
2 oz vodka
4 oz Bloody Mary mix *(pg 216)*
Garnish: lemon wedge, celery,
cocktail onion, you name it
*Variations: substitute gin for a **Red***
Snapper**, blanco tequila for a **Bloody Maria

FROZEN DAIQUIRI

"Constante" Vert, El Floridita | Havana | 1930s

BLEND | SNIFTER | SLUSH

¾ oz rich simple syrup
½ oz lime juice
1 ½ oz light Cuban-style rum
1 cup pebble ice

Garnish: lime wheel

FROZEN BANANA DAIQUIRI

Mountain Top | St. Thomas, USVI | 1950s

BLEND | SNIFTER | SLUSH

½ very ripe banana
½ oz rich demerara syrup
½ oz lime juice
1 oz crème de banane
1 oz aged Jamaican rum
1 oz light Cuban-style rum
1 ½ cups pebble ice

Garnish: cherry or banana dolphin

DAIQUIRI FRAPPÉ

"Constante" Vert, El Floridita | Havana | 1930s
Paul McGee, Lost Lake | Chicago | 2010s

BLEND | GEORGIAN | SLUSH

¼ tsp microplaned lime zest
1 ½ tbsp cane sugar
¾ oz lime juice
2 oz light Cuban-style rum
1 ½ cups pebble ice

Garnish: additional microplaned lime zest

FROZEN MARGARITA

unknown origin / 1930s

Mariano Martinez / Dallas / 1970s

BLEND | SNIFTER | SLUSH

¾ oz rich simple syrup

½ oz lime juice

1 ½ oz blanco tequila

1 cup pebble ice

Garnish: salted rim, lime wheel

Variation: substitute Tequila por mi Amante

FROZEN TOM STRAWBERRY

Dave Stolte / 2010s

BLEND | SNIFTER | SLUSH

4 frozen strawberries

½ oz rich simple syrup

½ oz lemon juice

1 ½ oz London Dry gin

1 cup pebble ice

Garnish: lemon wheel

DR. FRUNK

Dave Stolte / 2010s

BLEND | SNIFTER | SLUSH

1 tsp absinthe

½ oz rich simple syrup

½ oz grenadine

¾ oz lime juice

1 ½ oz Banks 5 rum

1 cup pebble ice

Garnish: lime wheel, mint sprig

¡PAPA DOBLE!

"Constante" Vert, El Floridita | Havana | 1930s
Allan Katz & Danielle Crouch, Jammyland
Las Vegas | 2010s

BLEND | DOUBLE ROCKS | SLUSH

scant 1 oz grapefruit cordial
¾ oz lime juice
1 ½ oz grapefruit juice
¼ oz maraschino liqueur
1 ½ oz light Cuban-style rum
1 ½ cups pebble ice

Garnish: grapefruit triangle & lime wheel

DIRTY BANANA

Natalie Jacob, Painkiller | New York | 2010s

BLEND | SNIFTER | SLUSH

½ very ripe banana
½ oz simple syrup
½ oz heavy cream
½ oz coffee liqueur
2 oz dark Jamaican rum
1 cup pebble ice

Garnish: orange & cherry flag

Grogs

Simple doesn't mean dumb. Two-ingredient Highballs, like any other drink, are done well when one pays attention to the details: measure your pours, use high-quality ingredients, and employ good ice. A common mistake home bartenders make is eyeballing proportions that will fill whatever glass is on hand. The usual Highball ratio is two ounces of booze with four ounces of lengthener. Ideally, you'll have dedicated Highball glasses around 10 ounces in capacity. Resist the urge to fill a bigger glass: either add more ice or just live with the glass not being full. The name "Highball" may have come from the Irish, who call for their drink of choice as a "ball o' malt" — so, simply a tall serving of whiskey ("boll" is Flemish for "glass" — the Dutch brought the term to England, along with their genever, then to Ireland). As far as we can tell, the original Highball was the Scotch & Soda, mixed in the UK with the carbonated water first manufactured by J.J. Schweppe in Geneva and London. With the popularity of sodas like ginger ale, Coca-Cola, and 7-Up in the late 19th and early 20th century, the Highball in all its forms became even more varied and accessible — and still reigns as the most popular style of mixed drink.

SCOTCH & SODA

London / 1860s

BUILD & STIR | HIGHBALL | ICE CUBES

2 oz blended Scotch whisky

4 oz seltzer

Express lemon oil over

Garnish: lemon twist

Alternative: Japanese whisky

GIN & TONIC

London / 1870s - 1900s

BUILD & STIR | HIGHBALL | ICE CUBES

2 oz Old Tom or London Dry gin

4 oz tonic soda

Express lemon oil over

Garnish: lemon twist

WHISKEY GINGER

London / 1870s

BUILD & STIR | HIGHBALL | ICE CUBES

2 oz Irish whiskey

4 oz ginger soda

Express lemon oil over

Garnish: lemon twist

VODKA SODA

New York / 1950s

BUILD & STIR | HIGHBALL | ICE CUBES

2 oz vodka

4 oz seltzer

Express lemon oil over

Garnish: lemon twist

PRESBYTERIAN

London / 1870s

BUILD & STIR | HIGHBALL | ICE CUBES

2 oz blended Scotch whisky

2 oz seltzer

2 oz ginger soda

Express lemon oil over

Garnish: lemon twist

GIN RICKEY

Shoemaker's / Washington DC / 1880s

BUILD & STIR | HIGHBALL | ICE CUBES

$1/4$ oz lime juice

2 oz London Dry gin

4 oz seltzer

Garnish: lime wedge

SCOTCH RICKEY

Shoemaker's / Washington DC / 1880s

BUILD & STIR | HIGHBALL | ICE CUBES

$1/4$ oz lime juice

2 oz blended Scotch whisky

4 oz seltzer

Garnish: lime wedge

MAMIE TAYLOR

Rochester, New York / 1890s

BUILD & STIR | HIGHBALL | ICE CUBES

$1/2$ oz lime juice

2 oz blended Scotch whisky

4 oz ginger soda

Garnish: lemon twist

HORSE'S NECK

Atlantic City | 1900s

BUILD & STIR | HIGHBALL | ICE CUBES

2 oz brandy or bourbon whiskey

4 oz ginger soda

Express lemon oil over

Garnish: long lemon twist

CABLEGRAM

New York | 1900s

BUILD & STIR | HIGHBALL | ICE CUBES

½ oz lime juice

2 oz rye whiskey

4 oz ginger soda

Garnish: candied ginger

CHILCANO

Peru | 1930s

BUILD & STIR | HIGHBALL | ICE CUBES

½ oz lime juice

2 oz pisco

4 oz ginger soda

Garnish: lime twist

DARK 'N' STORMY

Bermuda | 1920s

BUILD & STIR | HIGHBALL | ICE CUBES

½ oz lime juice

2 oz Gosling's Black Seal rum

4 oz ginger soda

Garnish: lime wedge

MOSCOW MULE

Cock 'n' Bull Tavern | Los Angeles | 1950s

WHIP | HIGHBALL | ICE CUBES

½ oz lime juice

2 oz vodka

4 oz ginger soda

Garnish: lime wedge, mint sprig

JACK & COKE

Tennessee | 1900s

BUILD & STIR | HIGHBALL | ICE CUBES

2 oz Tennessee whiskey

4 oz Coca-Cola

Express lemon oil over

Garnish: lemon twist

RUM & COKE

Havana | 1900s

BUILD & STIR | HIGHBALL | ICE CUBES

2 oz light Cuban-style rum

4 oz Coca-Cola

Express lemon oil over

Garnish: lemon twist

CUBA LIBRE

Havana | 1900s

BUILD & STIR | HIGHBALL | ICE CUBES

½ oz lime juice

2 oz light Cuban-style rum

4 oz Coca-Cola

Garnish: lime wheel

CUBA LIBRE PREPARADO

Venezuela / 1910s

BUILD & STIR | COLLINS | ICE CUBES

2 dashes Angostura bitters

½ oz lime juice

½ oz London Dry gin

1 ½ oz light Cuban-style rum

3 oz Coca-Cola

Garnish: lime wheel

BATANGA

Don Javier Delgado Corona, La Capilla
Tequila / 1950s

BUILD & STIR | HIGHBALL | ICE CUBES

½ oz lime juice

2 oz blanco tequila

4 oz Coca-Cola

Garnish: lime wheel,
salted rim (optional)

LA PALOMA

Mexico / 1950s

BUILD & STIR | HIGHBALL | ICE CUBES

1 pinch kosher salt

½ oz lime juice

2 oz blanco tequila

4 oz grapefruit soda

Garnish: lime wheel

WRAY & TING

Jamaica | 1970s

BUILD & STIR | HIGHBALL | ICE CUBES

2 oz Wray & Nephew overproof rum

4 oz grapefruit soda

Express grapefruit oil over

Garnish: grapefruit twist

FERNET & COKE

Córdoba | 1980s

BUILD & STIR | HIGHBALL | ICE CUBES

1 ½ oz Fernet-Branca

3 oz Coca-Cola

Express lemon oil over

Garnish: lemon twist

PIMM'S CUP

Pimm's Oyster House, London | 1840s

SWIZZLE | HIGHBALL | PEBBLE ICE

2 oz Pimm's #1

4 oz lemon soda

Swizzle

Garnish: cucumber wheel,
lemon wedge, mint sprig

AMERICANO

Gaspare Campari's | Milan | 1860s

BUILD & STIR | HIGHBALL | ICE CUBES

1 ½ oz Campari

1 ½ oz sweet vermouth

3 oz seltzer

Garnish: orange wheel

APEROL SPRITZ

Veneto | 1950s

BUILD & STIR

WINE GLASS | ICE CUBES

1 oz seltzer

2 oz Aperol

3 oz prosecco

Garnish: orange wheel

ITALIAN SPRITZ

Agostino Perrone, Connaught Bar

London | 2000s

BUILD & STIR | HIGHBALL | ICE CUBES

1/2 oz Galliano

1 oz Aperol

3 oz prosecco

Garnish: orange twist,

lemon twist, berries

MILK OF MARSEILLE

traditional | Marseille | 1920s

BUILD & STIR | HIGHBALL | ICE CUBES

1 dash grenadine (optional)

1 oz Ricard

5 oz cold water

No garnish

There are few things more satisfying and comforting than a well-made Irish Coffee. Cool cream blends with hot coffee as you take that first sip, backed up by the nip of Irish whiskey and rich sugar. Perfect for a rainy afternoon pick-me-up or a turbo-charged dessert. I prefer the somewhat extravagant Redbreast 12 in this — it's an old-style Irish whiskey made in pot stills for a bit more body and funk than column-still whiskey. That extra bit of character stands up well when mixed with bold coffee. For the coffee, use the best you can produce with freshly-ground medium-to-dark roast beans. Use a French Press or a pour-over kit to make the coffee (drip coffee makers generally don't get the water hot enough to extract the best flavor). Brew it a bit on the strong side (and don't use a metal jigger to pour it). Sugar-wise, the extra bit of molasses in turbinado or demerara unifies the coffee and whiskey more harmoniously than white sugar. And for the whipped cream: sorry to say, but you gotta hand-whip it fresh. Canned whipped cream isn't the right texture, won't float on top, and has sweetness that will throw off the drink's balance. This one is a perfect example of how specific glassware makes a difference: Many places use a larger, handled 8.5-ounce glass that encourage a bit too much coffee in the mix. Better to buy a set of the 6-ounce Libbey #8054 "Georgian" glasses they used in the original (made during World War II at a coastal seaplane port) and at The Buena Vista in San Francisco (where they make up to 2,000 Irish Coffees a day).

IRISH COFFEE

Foynes Airport | Ireland | 1940s

BUILD & STIR | GEORGIAN | WARM

In a sealed jar, shake until thick but still pourable, then chill:

1 oz heavy cream

In a warmed Georgian glass, stir to combine:

2 teaspoons demerara sugar

1 ½ oz Irish whiskey

scant ½ cup strong, dark roast hot coffee

Top with the thickened heavy cream

SPANISH COFFEE

Huber's | Portland | 1970s

BUILD & STIR | GEORGIAN | WARM

In a sealed jar, shake until thick but still pourable, then chill:

1 oz heavy cream

Rim the glass with lemon and sugar, then add:

¼ oz Cointreau

¾ oz 151 Demerara rum

Using a match, carefully ignite the rum and Cointreau, slowly rotating the glass to briefly caramelize the sugar. To douse the flame, add:

1 ½ oz coffee liqueur

⅓ cup strong, dark roast hot coffee

Top with the thickened heavy cream and grated nutmeg

KEOKE COFFEE

Bully's Steakhouse | San Diego | 1970s

BUILD & STIR | GEORGIAN | WARM

In a sealed jar, shake until thick but still pourable, then chill:

1 oz heavy cream

In a warmed Georgian glass, stir to combine:

½ oz crème de cacao

½ oz coffee liqueur

½ oz brandy or cognac

scant ½ cup strong, dark roast hot coffee

Top with the thickened heavy cream and grated coffee bean

MEXICAN HOT CHOCOLATE

Traditional | Jalisco | 1900s
Dave Stolte | 2010s

BUILD & STIR | GEORGIAN | WARM

In a sealed jar, shake until thick but still pourable, then chill:

1 oz heavy cream
¼ tsp green Chartreuse

In a warmed Georgian glass, stir to combine:

2 tbsp Mexican Chocolate
      Ganache *(pg 217)*
¼ cup boiling water

Add:

½ tsp Cointreau
1 ½ oz añejo tequila

Top with the thickened Chartreuse heavy cream and a sprinkle of Mexican Spice Mix (pg 215)

Nogs

Here comes dessert! The family of Nogs traces its lineage back to medieval Europe, where warm milk was mixed with eggs, sack (a forerunner of modern sherry), bread scraps, and highly-prized elite spices like cinnamon and nutmeg in a drink called "posset" that formed a liquid part for drinking and a curdled, pudding-like part for eating. For hundreds of years, warm or cold egg and cream drinks spiced and spiked with wine, sherry, or beer were common. As the drink style migrated to Colonial America, distilled spirits like rum, then whiskey and brandy, became the norm. George Washington liked his Egg Nogs with a combination of rye whiskey, rum, and sherry — truly democratic! During the 19th century, stiffer drinks prevailed — so much so that when New York bartender Troy Alexander created his signature gin-based drink in honor of advertising model Phoebe Snow (who promoted the "clean-burning" coal used by the Delaware, Lackawanna, and Western Railroad), it was rejected by gender-fearing macho critics as only fit for women and children. As if men don't like dessert, too! Mid-century America, however, had no problem with comfort foods and sweetness — enthusiastically offering up pastel-tinted hits like the Grasshopper, Pink Squirrel, and Golden Cadillac. The Nog family quietly endures the march of time and culinary trends, most recently finding curious bartenders in Portland asking questions like "what happens if you put an egg in a Negroni?" Happiness, that's what.

ALEXANDER

Troy Alexander, Rector's | New York | 1910s

SHAKE | COUPE | NO ICE

1 oz crème de cacao

1 ½ oz London Dry gin

1 oz heavy cream

Garnish: nutmeg

BRANDY ALEXANDER

Savoy | London | 1930s

SHAKE | COUPE | NO ICE

1 oz crème de cacao

1 ½ oz cognac

1 oz heavy cream

Garnish: nutmeg

ALEJANDRO

Dave Stolte / 2010s

SHAKE | COUPE | NO ICE

¼ oz Ancho Reyes

¾ oz crème de cacao

1 ½ oz mezcal

1 oz heavy cream

Express orange oil over

Garnish: nutmeg

GRASSHOPPER

Leroux Liquor Company / Philadelphia / 1940s

SHAKE | COUPE | NO ICE

1 oz crème de menthe

1 ¼ oz crème de cacao

1 oz heavy cream

Garnish: clapped mint leaf

PINK SQUIRREL

Bryant Sharp, Bryant's Cocktail Lounge

Milwaukee / 1940s

SHAKE | COUPE | NO ICE

1 oz crème de noyeaux

1 oz crème de cacao

1 oz heavy cream

Garnish: nutmeg

GOLDEN CADILLAC

Poor Red's BBQ | El Dorado | 1950s

SHAKE | COUPE | NO ICE

1 oz Galliano
1 oz crème de cacao
1 oz heavy cream

Garnish: nutmeg

NUTS & BERRIES

Unknown origin | 1980s

SHAKE | COUPE | NO ICE

1 oz Frangelico
1 oz Chambord
1 oz heavy cream

Garnish: nutmeg

NUGGET

Dave Stolte | 2020s

SHAKE | COUPE | NO ICE

1 tsp peanut butter powder
1 oz crème de cacao
1 oz crème de banane
1 oz heavy cream

Garnish: shaved dark chocolate

HOOPER

Dave Stolte | 2020s

SHAKE | COUPE | NO ICE

2 tsp malted milk powder

½ oz vanilla syrup

½ oz crème de cacao

1 oz genever

1 oz heavy cream

Garnish: grated dark chocolate

SMITH & KEARNS

Gerbert "Shorty" Doebber, Blue Blazer
Bismarck | 1950s

SHAKE | HIGHBALL | ICE CUBES

2 oz coffee liqueur or crème de cacao

2 oz heavy cream

Add:

2 oz seltzer

No garnish

WHITE RUSSIAN

San Francisco | 1960s
Milk & Honey | New York | 2000s

STIR | COUPE | NO ICE

In a sealed jar, shake until thick but still
pourable, then set aside:

1 oz heavy cream

Stir:

1 ½ oz coffee liqueur

1 ½ oz vodka

Top with thickened heavy cream

Garnish: grated coffee bean

COLORADO BULLDOG

Unknown origin / 1970s

SHAKE | ROCKS | ICE CUBES

1 oz coffee liqueur

1 oz vodka

1 oz heavy cream

Carefully top with:

2 oz Coca-Cola

No garnish

MUDSLIDE

Old Judd, The Wreck Bar & Grill

Grand Cayman, BWI / 1950s

BLEND | DOUBLE ROCKS | SLUSH

1 ½ oz coffee liqueur

1 ½ oz Irish cream liqueur

1 ½ oz vodka

1 ½ cups pebble ice

Float:

2 tsp coffee liqueur

Garnish: grated cinnamon, cherry

FROZEN IRISH COFFEE

Erin Rose / New Orleans / 1970s

BLEND | DOUBLE ROCKS | SLUSH

1 tsp rich demerara syrup

2 oz brandy

2 oz coffee liqueur

4 oz chilled coffee

½ cup vanilla ice cream

1 ½ cups pebble ice

Garnish: grated coffee bean

BRANDY MILK PUNCH

England | 1500s
New Orleans | 1800s

DUMP | ROCKS | PEBBLE ICE

¾ oz vanilla syrup
2 oz cognac
2 oz whole milk
Garnish: nutmeg

NEW ORLEANS MILK PUNCH

New Orleans | 1800s

DUMP | ROCKS | PEBBLE ICE

¾ oz vanilla syrup
1 oz bourbon whiskey
1 oz aged Jamaican rum
2 oz whole milk
Garnish: nutmeg

BATIDA DE COCA

traditional | Brazil | 1930s

BLEND | SNIFTER | SLUSH

1 ½ oz coconut syrup
1 oz sweetened condensed milk
2 oz cachaça
1 cup pebble ice
Garnish: nutmeg

PIÑA COLADA

Ramón "Monchito" Marrero
Caribe Hilton | San Juan, Puerto Rico | 1950s
BLEND | SNIFTER | SLUSH

1 oz coconut syrup
4 one-inch chunks pineapple
¼ oz lime juice
2 oz light Cuban-style rum
1 cup pebble ice
Garnish: orange & cherry flag

PAINKILLER

Daphne Henderson, Soggy Dollar Bar
Jost van Dyke, BVI | 1970s
SHAKE | DOUBLE ROCKS | PEBBLE ICE

1 oz coconut syrup
1 oz orange juice
2 oz pineapple juice
2 oz Denizen
    Merchant's Reserve rum
Garnish: orange & cherry flag

SKY JUICE

Goldie's Conch House
Nassau, Bahamas | 1990s
SHAKE | COLLINS | ICE CUBES

⅛ teaspoon freshly grated nutmeg
1 oz sweetened condensed milk
2 oz London Dry gin
4 oz coconut milk
Garnish: nutmeg

BOSOM CARESSER

London / 1910s

SHAKE | COUPE | NO ICE

Dry shake, then add ice and shake again:

1 egg yolk

¼ oz grenadine

½ oz rainwater Madeira

½ oz Grand Marnier

1 oz cognac

Garnish: cherry

BOSTON FLIP

Colonial America / 1750s

SHAKE | COUPE | NO ICE

Dry shake, then add ice and shake again:

¼ oz rich demerara syrup

1 egg

1 ½ oz rainwater Madeira

1 ½ oz rye whiskey

Garnish: nutmeg

WHISKEY FLIP

Colonial America / 1750s

SHAKE | COUPE | NO ICE

Dry shake, then add ice and shake again:

¼ oz rich demerara syrup

1 egg

2 oz bourbon whiskey

Garnish: nutmeg

COFFEE FLIP

Jerry Thomas | 1860s (as "Coffee Cocktail")

SHAKE | COUPE | NO ICE

Dry shake, then add ice and shake again:

¼ oz rich demerara syrup

1 egg

1 ½ oz ruby Port

1 ½ oz cognac

Garnish: nutmeg

CYNAR FLIP

Ben Sandrof, Clyde Common | Portland | 2010s

SHAKE | COUPE | NO ICE

Dry shake, then add ice and shake again:

¼ oz rich demerara syrup

1 egg

2 oz Cynar

Garnish: Angostura bitters décor

NEGRONI FLIP

Kask | Portland | 2010s

SHAKE | COUPE | NO ICE

Dry shake, then add ice and shake again:

¼ oz rich simple syrup

1 egg

1 oz Campari

1 oz sweet vermouth

1 oz London Dry gin

Garnish: orange twist

If you only know Egg Nog from the grocery-store cartons, and have perhaps rejected it as mysterious, coagulated, syrupy, and strange, you're in for a treat. When made fresh, it's light and comforting — just bourbon and nutmeg create that familiar "what is that?" Egg Nog flavor. But you might be surprised to know that prior to the middle of the 20th century, Egg Nog was always aged. Sometimes just a few days, but anywhere up to six months was common. I hear the panic now about drinking milk and raw eggs past their expiration date. Be assured that smart food scientists have thoroughly tested the process and found that an immersion in beverage alcohol for three weeks is adequate to kill all foodborne pathogens that may have been present in the milk and eggs (and is the sweet spot in terms of flavor). So not only is it unexpectedly safe, refrigerator-aged Egg Nog also transforms in the drinking experience, becoming more supple and enhancing unexpected flavor notes like mint. Innovative Portland bartender Jeffrey Morgenthaler, always looking for efficient production methods, pioneered the technique of using an electric blender to combine and aerate the drink. He also found the intriguing combination of Amontillado sherry and añejo tequila work exceptionally well in place of the traditional bourbon, creating a rich, nutty connection to the nutmeg. A mix of brandy and rum takes the drink back to Colonial America. You're encouraged to experiment and find your own holiday tradition, aged or not.

EGG NOG

Europe | 1500s
Jeffrey Morgenthaler, Clyde Common
Portland | 2000s
BLEND | PUNCH CUP | NO ICE
4 eggs
Blend on high one minute, then add:
1 cup white sugar
Continue blending to mix, then add:
1 teaspoon freshly grated nutmeg
1 cup bourbon whiskey
1 cup heavy cream
1 ½ cups whole milk
Keep refrigerated
Garnish: nutmeg
Variation: blend of 4 oz añejo tequila
& 5 oz amontillado sherry
MAKES 1 ½ QUARTS / SERVES 8

TOM & JERRY

Colonial America | 1800s
Andrew Bohrer | Seattle | 2010s
BUILD & STIR | GEORGIAN | WARM
1 tbsp Tom & Jerry batter *(pg 216)*
1 oz cognac
1 oz dark Jamaican rum
2 oz warm whole milk
Stir to blend.
Garnish: nutmeg

COQUITO

San Juan | 1800s
Giuseppe González | New York | 2000s
BUILD & STIR | PUNCH CUP | NO ICE
In a pot over low heat, stir:
1/2 tsp ground nutmeg
2 tsp vanilla extract
2 tsp ground cinnamon
12 oz coconut syrup
28 oz sweetened
    condensed milk (2 cans)
24 oz evaporated milk (2 cans)
Simmer gently for five minutes, whisking to
blend spices. Let cool, then add:
1 1/2 cups aged Puerto Rican rum
Transfer to bottles and add a cinnamon stick
to each bottle; keep refrigerated
Garnish: grated cinnamon
MAKES 5 17-OZ BOTTLES / SERVES 20

HOT BUTTERED RUM

Colonial America | 1650s
Traditional adaptation | Seattle | 1970s
BUILD & STIR | GEORGIAN | WARM
Stir to combine:
1 tbsp Hot Buttered Rum batter *(pg 217)*
¼ cup boiling water
Optional emulsifier (pg 217):
separately, at room temperature,
stir to combine, then add to the
hot mixture:
½ tsp Ticaloid 210S

1 ½ oz Plantation OFTD rum
Stir to blend
Garnish: nutmeg

ABSINTHE SUISSESSE

New Orleans | 1910s
Chris Hannah, Arnaud's French 75
New Orleans | 2010s
SHAKE | GEORGIAN | NO ICE
Briefly dry shake:
1 egg white
¼ oz orgeat
½ oz Herbsaint

½ oz crème de menthe
1 oz absinthe
1 oz half and half
Add ice and shake again, then double-strain
Garnish: mint sprig

STROH WITH THE FLOW

Beth Harding, Hale Pele | Portland | 2010s

FLASH BLEND | ROCKS | PEBBLE ICE

¼ ripe banana
½ oz coconut syrup
1 oz pineapple juice
¾ oz dark Jamaican rum
¾ oz Stroh 160
½ cup pebble ice

Garnish: pineapple spear, nutmeg

IRISH GOODBYE

Erick Castro | San Diego | 2010s

SHAKE | COUPE | NO ICE

Briefly dry shake:
1 whole egg
½ oz maple syrup
1 oz Averna
1 oz Irish whiskey
1 oz heavy cream

*Add ice and shake again,
then double-strain*
Garnish: grated cinnamon

Lagniappe

*New Orleans has a wonderful tradition: the
lagniappe (lan-yap). It's a French Cajun word
meaning "a little something extra." Could be a bite
of dessert or a digestivo brought out on the house.
The idea is, no matter how done you are, there's
always room for "just a taste more." A cheeky
half-portion of any Nog from the previous section
makes for a fine Lagniappe. Above and beyond,
here's a handful of some of our favorite little
somethings to see you off to bed... but please get
home safely and don't go too far.*

FAITH IN MEDICINE

Jason Schiffer, 320 Main | Seal Beach | 2010s

NEAT | CABALLITO | NO ICE

Layer:

1 oz falernum

1 oz Angostura bitters

Drink in one shot

HARD START

Damon Boelte, Prime Meats | New York | 2000s

NEAT | CABALLITO | NO ICE

1 oz Fernet-Branca

1 oz Branca Menta

FERRARI

New York | 2000s

NEAT | CABALLITO | NO ICE

1 oz Fernet-Branca

1 oz Campari

THE JIMBO

Jimmy Palumbo, Extra Fancy
Williamsburg | 2010s
NEAT | CABALLITO | NO ICE
1 oz Meletti
1 oz rye whiskey

TRASH & MONEY

Half Step | Austin | 2010s
NEAT | CABALLITO | NO ICE
1 oz Green Chartreuse
1 oz mezcal

CHINA SYNDROME

David Kupchinsky | The Eveleigh | 2010s
NEAT | CABALLITO | NO ICE
1 oz Cynar
1 oz bonded rye whiskey

M&M

Marco Montefiori | 2010s
NEAT | CABALLITO | NO ICE
1 oz Amaro Montenegro
1 oz mezcal

CAFFÈ PAZZO

Dave Castillo | 2010s
NEAT | CABALLITO | NO ICE
1 oz Amaro Sfumato
1 ¼ oz St. George NOLA
    coffee liqueur

O.F. SLUG

Jason Schiffer, 320 Main | Seal Beach | 2010s

NEAT | CABALLITO | NO ICE

4 dashes Angostura bitters

1 tsp rich demerara syrup

2 oz rye whiskey

NO BABIES

San Francisco | 2010s

NEAT | CABALLITO | NO ICE

1 pinch kosher salt

1 oz Cynar

1 oz straight apple brandy

BITTERS & SODA

Traditional | 1830s

BUILD | ROCKS | PEBBLE ICE

12 dashes Angostura bitters

6 oz seltzer

Express lemon oil over

Garnish: lemon twist

THE FUTURE FAVOR

NEAT | COLLINS | NO ICE

10 oz water

Drink two servings,

then finish with:

2 Tylenol

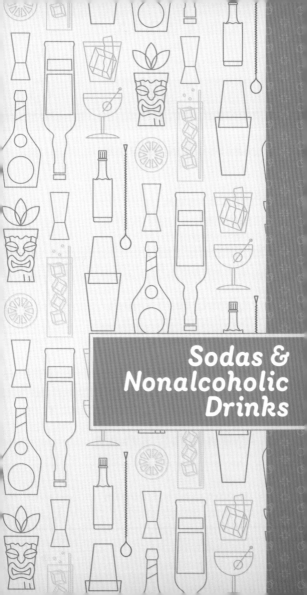

Sodas & Nonalcoholic Drinks

TONIC SODA

England | 1850s

BUILD & STIR
HIGHBALL | ICE CUBES
1 oz tonic syrup
4 oz seltzer

GINGER SODA

Yorkshire | 1750s
Belfast | 1850s

BUILD & STIR
HIGHBALL | ICE CUBES
1 oz ginger syrup
1 oz lemon juice
4 oz seltzer

LEMON SODA

Paris | 1830s

BUILD & STIR
HIGHBALL | ICE CUBES
1 oz lemon syrup
1 oz lemon juice
4 oz seltzer

ORANGE SODA

San Francisco | 1890s

BUILD & STIR
HIGHBALL | ICE CUBES
1 oz orange syrup
1 oz orange juice
4 oz seltzer

LEMON-LIME SODA

St. Louis / 1920s

BUILD & STIR | HIGHBALL | ICE CUBES

1 oz lemon-lime syrup
½ oz lemon juice
½ oz lime juice
4 oz seltzer

GRAPEFRUIT SODA

Phoenix / 1930s

BUILD & STIR | HIGHBALL | ICE CUBES

1 oz grapefruit syrup or cordial
1 oz grapefruit juice
4 oz seltzer

SPARKLING FRUIT PUNCH

California / 1940s

BUILD & STIR | HIGHBALL | ICE CUBES

1 oz fassionola
½ oz pineapple juice
½ oz orange juice
4 oz seltzer

CITRUS SELTZER

Unknown origin

BUILD & STIR | HIGHBALL | ICE CUBES

*Express oil from two citrus twists
into the glass, add ice and:*
6 oz seltzer

CREAM SODA

Massachusetts / 1850s

BUILD & STIR | HIGHBALL | NO ICE

In a sealed jar, shake until thick but still pourable, then chill:

1 oz heavy cream

In a chilled glass, add:

8 oz cold soda (your choice)

Combine, then float:

½ oz vanilla syrup

2 oz heavy cream

Garnish: thickened heavy cream

SHIRLEY TEMPLE

Chasen's, Beverly Hills / 1930s

BUILD & STIR

HIGHBALL | ICE CUBES

½ oz grenadine

4 oz ginger soda

Garnish: cherries

ROY ROGERS

Unknown origin / 1940s

BUILD & STIR

HIGHBALL | ICE CUBES

½ oz grenadine

4 oz Coca-Cola

Garnish: cherries

LEMONADE

traditional

BUILD & STIR | HIGHBALL | ICE CUBES

In a pitcher, create an oleosaccharum (pg 74):

Peels of 6 lemons

1 cup superfine white sugar

Add the following, then remove peels:

1 ½ cups lemon juice

6 cups water

Variations:

Add ¼ oz grenadine for **Pink Lemonade**,

serve 50/50 with iced tea as an **Arnold Palmer**

MAKES 2 QUARTS / SERVES 8

HORCHATA

traditional / Mexico

Jeffrey Morgenthaler, Clyde Common

Portland / 2000s

BLEND | HIGHBALL | ICE CUBES

Combine and soak overnight:

3 sticks cinnamon, crumbled

1 cup white sugar

3 cups long-grain white rice

1 cup raw almonds, chopped

6 cups hot water

(Optional emulsifier, pg 217:

after its overnight soak, add:

2 tsp Ticaloid 210S*

Blend until smooth, scrape through a sieve,

then squeeze through a nut milk bag or several

layers of cheesecloth; keep refrigerated

MAKES 1 QUART / SERVES 4

SWITCHEL

traditional | Colonial Caribbean & US | 1680s
Dave Stolte & Jason Schiffer | 2020s
BLEND | HIGHBALL | ICE CUBES
Blend until smooth:
1/4 tsp kosher salt
6 oz fresh ginger, chopped
1/2 cup unfiltered apple cider vinegar
3 tbsp pure maple syrup
3 tsp molasses
1 tbsp lemon juice
4 cups water
Blend until smooth, strain through a sieve,
then through a nut milk bag or several layers
of cheesecloth; keep refrigerated
Garnish: mint sprig
MAKES 2 QUARTS / SERVES 8

SANDÍA AGUA FRESCA

traditional | Tenochtitlán | 1320s
BLEND | HIGHBALL | ICE CUBES
Blend until smooth:
4 cups chopped, seeded watermelon
1 tbsp sugar
3 tsp lime juice
1 1/2 cups water
Strain, then add an additional:
1 1/2 cups water
Keep refrigerated
Garnish: mint sprig
MAKES 2 QUARTS / SERVES 8

SERGIO LEONE

Jason Schiffer / 2010s

BUILD & STIR | COLLINS | ICE CUBES

½ oz cold coffee

4 oz Sanpellegrino
Aranciata Rosso

Garnish: lemon twist & mint sprig

COCONUTEA

Jason Schiffer / 2010s

BUILD & STIR | COLLINS | ICE CUBES

3 oz coconut water

3 oz cold green tea

Garnish: grated nutmeg & mint sprig

SPRAY TAN

Jim Meehan,
American Express Centurion Lounge LAX / 2010s

BUILD & STIR

COLLINS | ICE CUBES

2 oz Seedlip Spice 94

4 oz Crodino

Garnish: orange half-wheel

PARADISI SPRITZ

Dave Stolte / 2020s

BUILD & STIR | COLLINS | ICE CUBES

Express grapefruit oil from a large
twist into the glass, then add:

2 oz Sanbitter

4 oz seltzer

Garnish: grapefruit twist

SPARKLING ALMOND

Erick Castro, Polite Provisions
San Diego | 2010s

BUILD & STIR | COLLINS | ICE CUBES

1 ½ oz orgeat
1 oz lemon juice
4 oz seltzer

Garnish: lemon wheel & mint sprig
Note: the orgeat recipe in this book
contains a very small amount of vodka
as a preservative

WEAKY TIKI

Michelle Bearden, 320 Main
Seal Beach | 2010s

DUMP | SNIFTER | PEBBLE ICE

¼ oz cinnamon syrup
½ oz rich demerara syrup
½ oz pineapple juice
¾ oz lime juice
¾ oz grapefruit juice
2 oz water

Garnish: nutmeg & mint sprig

Prep

A quick note on safety:
When storing syrups and cordials, you'll want to keep an eye out for spoilage. Look for a change in the clarity of the mix or for unwanted growies or floaties. Pure syrups (just sugar and water) are unlikely to spoil unless their storage vessel is tainted. When you start adding other ingredients, it's a good practice to add an ounce of 50% ABV vodka to help inhibit spoilage. Liqueurs, having a spirit base rather than water or juice, are less likely to go bad.

SIMPLE SYRUP really is simple. In an airtight jar, mix one cup of white sugar with one cup of water, shaking well to blend, then let it sit for several hours or overnight to completely dissolve. Give it a few brisk shakes to encourage it as it goes along. This is referred to as the "cold method" and retains the brightness of white sugar. Keep refrigerated. Will last about six months.

For **RICH SIMPLE SYRUP**, use one cup of sugar to a half-cup of water. Same process as regular simple syrup, but will require more shaking to combine. Keep refrigerated. Will last about six months.

RICH DEMERARA SYRUP can be heated gently to combine faster without negatively impacting the flavor. Cook one cup of demerara sugar (turbinado sugar is an acceptable substitute) with a half-cup of water over low heat, stirring until the sugar is dissolved. Keep refrigerated. Will last about six months.

HONEY SYRUP keeps honey from freezing and seizing when mixed in cocktails. Mix three-quarters of a cup honey with one quarter of a cup of boiling water and stir to combine. Add one ounce of 50% ABV vodka. Keep refrigerated. Will last about three months.

GINGER SYRUP can also be the sweet kick in delicious nonalcoholic sodas, in addition to use in cocktails. I like Jeffrey Morgenthaler's easy method: in a blender, combine one cup chopped ginger with one cup boiling water and one cup white sugar. Purée until smooth (secure the lid with a dishtowel to avoid a steam-pressure disaster). Strain through several layers of cheesecloth or a nut milk bag to remove any fine particles. Add one ounce of 50% ABV vodka. Keep refrigerated. Will last about three months. Shake before using.

ORGEAT (*or-zhat*) is a floral almond syrup, originally from the Middle East. In a heavyweight Ziploc bag or wrapped in a clean dishtowel, smash two and a half cups of whole, raw almonds — just enough to break them into large chunks, not pulverized. A mallet or a rolling pin works well. Arrange almonds in a single layer on an ungreased baking sheet (use parchment paper if you like) and toast in a preheated oven at 400° for 10 minutes. In a saucepan, combine the toasted almonds with two cups of sugar and one and a half cups of water. Bring to a simmer over low heat, then cook 10 minutes, stirring to dissolve the sugar. Remove from the heat and let cool, then pour into an airtight container and let the mixture steep, unrefrigerated, for 24 hours. Strain the mixture through several layers of cheesecloth or a nut milk bag into your storage vessel (it'll take a while to slowly drip out), then add 12 drops of orange flower water, 12 drops of rosewater, and one ounce of 50% ABV vodka. Shake to blend. Keep refrigerated. Will last about one year.

CINNAMON SYRUP starts with toasting three cinnamon sticks in a saucepan over low heat, crushed lightly. When you can smell the cinnamon toasting and see a bit of steam escaping, remove from the heat. Crush them again, just into a few more pieces, but don't pulverize. Into the saucepan with cinnamon, add one and a half cups of white sugar and one and a half cups of water, then simmer over low heat for 10 minutes, stirring to dissolve sugar. Cool, then pour into an airtight glass container and let steep, refrigerated, overnight. Strain into your storage vessel through several layers of cheesecloth or a nut milk bag to remove fine particles. Add one ounce of 50% ABV vodka. Keep refrigerated. Will last about one year.

To make **VANILLA SYRUP**, split two vanilla beans lengthwise and scrape out the seeds. Over medium-low heat, mix one cup of white sugar with one cup of water, stirring until sugar is dissolved. Add the vanilla seeds and bean pods, whisking to distribute evenly. Simmer on low heat for 10 minutes. Cool, then pour into an airtight glass container and let steep, refrigerated, overnight. Strain into your storage vessel through several layers of cheesecloth or a nut milk bag to remove fine particles. Add one ounce of 50% ABV vodka. Keep refrigerated. Will last about three months.

The recipe for **CITRUS SYRUP** works with lemon, lime, orange, grapefruit, or a lemon-lime combo, and it starts with an oleosaccharum. In a bowl, rub the zests of your chosen citrus (either four lemons, six limes, three oranges, two grapefruits, or a combination of two lemons and four limes) with one cup of superfine sugar. Let rest approximately four hours, stirring occasionally, until the sugar is dissolved and the citrus oils are extracted. When ready, combine the oleosaccharum with a half-cup of water and cook, stirring, over low heat just until the oleosaccharum has integrated. Remove the citrus twists, then add a half-teaspoon of citric acid and stir to combine. Add one ounce of 50% ABV vodka. Keep refrigerated. Will last about three months.

Homemade **COCONUT SYRUP** avoids the "suntan lotion" essence of commercial products. In a blender, combine one cup of canned coconut milk with one cup of white sugar. Blend to combine, then add one ounce of 50% ABV vodka. Keep refrigerated. Will last about three months.

PASSION FRUIT SYRUP is a bright taste of the tropics. In a saucepan, combine one cup of frozen passion fruit purée with one cup of white sugar and cook, stirring, over low heat just until the sugar has dissolved. Let cool, then add one ounce of 50% ABV vodka. Keep refrigerated. Will last about three months.

FASSIONOLA, a somewhat obscure tropical syrup, also makes for a delicious soda. In a saucepan, combine one and a half cups of white sugar, one cup of water, and one cup of dried hibiscus blossoms and stir over very low heat until sugar is dissolved. Remove from the heat and let the mixture steep for one hour, then discard the hibiscus blossoms. In a blender, combine the hibiscus syrup with one cup of frozen passion fruit pulp, a half-cup of fresh or frozen pineapple chunks, one tablespoon of frozen guava pulp, four strawberries (fresh or frozen), two raspberries (fresh or frozen), a half-teaspoon of almond extract, and a half-teaspoon of citric acid. Blend until smooth. Fine strain to remove strawberry seeds and any bits of pulp. Add one ounce of 50% ABV vodka. Keep refrigerated. Will last about three months.

GRENADINE, the real kind, is miles above the typical turbo-red artificial goop. Mix one cup of unsweetened pomegranate juice (POM is preferred) with one cup of white sugar. Cook over low heat, stirring until the sugar is dissolved. When it's cool, add one-and-a-half teaspoons of orange flower water and one ounce of 50% ABV vodka. Keep refrigerated. Will last about six months.

LIME CORDIAL is Jason Schiffer's homemade, fresh, and far-superior replacement for Rose's Lime Juice. Start by grating the zest of five limes and chopping a half-cup of ginger (no need to peel the ginger). Set aside. After zesting, juice the limes and strain through a fine-mesh strainer, to yield one and a half cups, juicing more limes if necessary to make that volume. In a saucepan over medium heat, combine the lime juice with one and a half cups of white sugar. Watch and

stir regularly to dissolve the sugar. Remove the saucepan from heat just before it comes to a boil. Rest the hot mixture for five minutes, then add the reserved lime zest and ginger. Let it infuse for 20 minutes, then strain through a fine-mesh strainer into your storage vessel. Add one ounce of 50% ABV vodka. Keep refrigerated. Will last about three months.

This **GRAPEFRUIT CORDIAL** recipe comes from Jammyland in Las Vegas, where the locals love it in a frozen Papa Doble and other tropical drinks. To start, peel one quarter of a Ruby Red grapefruit, then roughly chop the peeled grapefruit into chunks. In a saucepan, add the peel and chopped grapefruit to two cups of freshly-squeezed juice from additional grapefruit. Bring this to a boil, then lower to a gentle simmer and slightly reduce, about 10 percent. Fine-strain the juice, then whisk in two cups of white sugar until dissolved. Add one half-ounce of Wray & Nephew overproof Jamaican rum. Keep refrigerated. Will last about four weeks.

LIQUEURS

FALERNUM is a spiced rum liqueur originally from Barbados. This recipe is inspired by Paul Clarke's "Falernum #10." In a saucepan over medium heat, lightly toast 50 cloves, one tablespoon whole allspice berries, and one whole nutmeg (crushed, not ground). In an airtight container,

combine with a cup of aged 151 Spanish-style rum, the peeled zest from 8 limes (being careful to not include any of the bitter white pith), and a half-cup of grated fresh ginger. Infuse for 24 hours, then fine-strain the infused rum to remove ingredients and small particles. Make a rich simple syrup of two cups white sugar and one cup water and let cool. In an airtight container, combine the infused rum, the rich simple syrup, and 10 drops of almond extract. Stir to combine. Let it rest two weeks, refrigerated, for the ginger to mellow. Keep refrigerated. Will last about 12 months. Shake before using.

PIMENTO DRAM, sometimes called Allspice Liqueur, is named for *Pimenta dioica*, the Jamaica Pepper tree. Confusing, but no relation to the cherry-pepper chiles that get stuffed into olives. To make this tiki essential, lightly toast a quarter-cup of whole dried allspice berries in a saucepan over low heat just until fragrant, then lightly crush — just enough to break them into chunks, not pulverized. In an airtight container, combine the allspice with one cup plus one ounce of aged 151 Spanish-style rum. Let the mixture steep for 10 days in a cool, dark place. Strain the infused rum through several layers of cheesecloth or a nut milk bag, then through a paper coffee filter to remove fine particles. In a saucepan over medium-low heat, combine one and a half cups of water with two and a half cups of light brown sugar. Stir to blend until sugar is completely dissolved. Let the syrup cool, then add the infused rum. Funnel into an airtight glass bottle or jar and let it rest 30 days, refrigerated, to level out the heat of the allspice. Keep refrigerated. Will last indefinitely.

LIMONCELLO is a delicious dessert indulgence originally from the Amalfi coast of Italy, and couldn't be simpler. The late food historian Ernest Miller taught me his technique, easy to remember since it's all about "the ones." Peel one pound of lemons, being careful to avoid any white pith. In a one-quart jar, combine the peels with one 750 mL bottle of 50% ABV vodka. Cover tightly and let rest in a cool, dark place for one month. Discard the peels and measure the volume of the infused spirit (some may have been lost to evaporation in spite of the lid). Make a batch of simple syrup (one part white sugar, one part water) equal to the amount of the infused spirit. Let the simple syrup cool and then combine with the infused spirit. Portion the limoncello into bottles and keep in the freezer. Will last indefinitely. Makes great gifts, and works well with other citrus too.

NOCINO is an Italian walnut liqueur, traditionally made in June and enjoyed during the holidays in December. This recipe comes courtesy of Louis Anderman at Miracle Mile Bitters. The first step is to locate seasonal green, unripe walnuts at the end of May or the first week of June. I order online from Mount Lassen Farms in California — but also check for local sources near you. In Italy, nocino is traditionally started on June 24, St. John's Day. Do with that information what you will, but plan to start your batch in late June. Be ready with a three-liter airtight lidded glass jar. Get out your crappiest cutting board and put on disposable gloves (green walnuts will stain things black), then, using a sturdy and sharp knife, slice each walnut in half. Pile the walnuts into the jar, then add two cups of demerara sugar, two sticks of cinnamon, seven whole cloves, one star anise pod, one vanilla bean (sliced in two lengthwise), and the zests of one large lemon and one small orange. Pour in one 750 mL bottle of 50% ABV vodka (not the lower-powered regular 40% stuff) and one 375 mL bottle of grappa. Close the lid and give it a good hard shake to start dissolving the sugar. You'll need to shake it daily for the first week to get the sugar completely dissolved. Find a sunny spot in your kitchen, or wherever you like, and let it sit for 40 days. Set a reminder in your calendar. You'll see the liquid start to turn a weird dark forest green color, then go black as night. All the while, those walnuts are giving up their deep richness and getting to know the spices they're soaking with. After 40 days, strain out and discard the walnuts and spices. Strain the nocino three times through coffee filters until there's no visible sediment left, and then portion it into bottles. Set it aside until December, if you can wait that long. The flavors will continue to change and evolve over years, if you can make it last. Enjoy in cocktails or neat at room temperature.

INFUSED & BLENDED SPIRITS

TEQUILA POR MI AMANTE should probably be called *Tequila con Fresas,* but its incorrectly-translated name ("tequila because of my lover") was standardized by bon vivant and author Charles

Baker in his 1939 *Gentleman's Companion*, so now we're stuck with it. In an airtight container, combine one 750 mL bottle of blanco tequila with three pints of ripe, organic, strawberries that have been washed and hulled (large ones get sliced in half). Reserve the empty tequila bottle. Seal the container and allow to steep in the refrigerator three weeks, gently agitating occasionally. After three weeks, strain the mixture through a fine-mesh strainer, then a nut milk bag or cheesecloth into the reserved tequila bottle. Keep refrigerated. Will last three months. You may see some coagulated natural pectin from the strawberries collecting as a gummy cloud in the bottle — just give it a shake before using.

Historian and author Wayne Curtis has created a great approximation for the elusive **PEACH BRANDY** found in 17th- and 18th-century recipes. In an empty 750 mL bottle, combine a half-cup of crème de peche, a half-cup of vodka, a three-quarter cup of straight apple brandy, and a three-

quarter cup of cognac with 10 drops of almond extract. Label to avoid confusion. Will keep at room temperature indefinitely.

This **SPICED RUM**, developed by bartenders Paul McGee and David Hridel, will send the dread Captain Morgan straight to Davey Jones' Locker. In a saucepan, lightly toast one whole nutmeg (crushed, not ground), one cinnamon stick (broken up), one vanilla bean (cut lengthwise and then into three sections), two whole cloves, one cardamom pod (lightly crushed), four black peppercorns, one star anise, and three allspice berries. Let the spice mixture go just until you smell it toasting, then briefly pulverize the mix in a clean coffee grinder or with a mortar and pestle. Peel one large navel orange, taking care to not include too much pith. In a one-quart glass jar, combine all ingredients with a 750 mL bottle of aged Spanish-style rum (reserve the empty bottle) and cover tightly. Shake to blend, then let it rest in a cool, dark place for 24 hours, shaking a few times as it infuses. Strain the spiced rum through several layers of cheesecloth or a nut milk bag to remove any fine particles, then return it to the original bottle; label to avoid confusion. Will keep at room temperature indefinitely, although the spice level may fade after a few months. Enjoy neat, over ice, or in cocktails like an Old Fashioned.

ROCK & RYE was a popular 19th-century ready-to-drink cocktail. It was originally made with rock sugar candy, but the hassle and waste of making rock candy isn't actually necessary (unless you feel like taking on a science experiment just for kicks). In a one-quart glass jar, combine 750 mL of rye whiskey (reserve the bottle), three ounces of superfine sugar, cover tightly, and shake well until the sugar is dissolved. Add three orange twists, three lemon twists, four dried apricots, and eight dried Montmorency cherries. Let it rest in a cool, dark place for three days, shaking a few times as it infuses. After three days, add two whole cloves, two cinnamon sticks, and one teaspoon of dried horehound. Let it rest in a cool, dark place an additional 24 hours, shaking now and again. Strain through several layers of cheesecloth or a nut milk bag to remove any fine particles, then funnel it back into the original bottle and label it to avoid confusion. Will keep at room temperature indefinitely, although you may notice the spice level fading after a few months. Enjoy over ice.

Homemade **COCKTAIL ONIONS** are
a snap to make, no harder than quick
refrigerator pickles. Trim the root ends
from eight ounces of fresh (not frozen)
pearl onions. In rolling boiling water,
blanch the onions for one minute, let cool
briefly, then remove the outer skins by
squeezing the onions from the stem end
to pop them out. A totally optional next
step (but recommended, if you're able)
is to lightly smoke the cocktail onions
on your grill. Ensure the onions are dry,
then add them to a foil pie pan in a single
layer. Smoke over very low, indirect heat
for about 20 minutes, stirring a few times.
I've found alder or oak wood smoke is
particularly nice. Now, add the onions
(smoked or otherwise) to a clean eight-oz
Mason jar, then prepare a brine of:

¼ cup sherry vinegar
¼ cup apple cider vinegar
¼ cup water
½ tbsp kosher salt
⅛ cup white sugar
¼ tsp whole mustard seed
¼ tsp celery seed
½ tsp whole peppercorns
¼ tsp red pepper flakes
1 sprig fresh rosemary

Bring the brine to a boil, stirring until the sugar dissolves. Remove the rosemary stem then pour the hot brine into the jar to cover the onions. Let cool, then seal and refrigerate. Will keep approximately two months.

CANDIED GINGER makes for a delicious garnish — if it doesn't all get eaten first. Coat a wire rack with non-stick spray, then set the rack into a sheet pan lined with parchment paper. Using the side of a spoon, peel one pound of fresh ginger, then slice into one-eighth-inch-thick slices. In a saucepan, combine the ginger with five cups of water. Cook, covered, over medium-high heat for half an hour or until the ginger softens. When ready, drain the water, reserving one-quarter cup. Return the ginger and the quarter-cup of water to the pan then add two cups of sugar. Bring to a low boil over medium-high heat, stirring to dissolve, then to begin drying out, the syrup. After 20 minutes, you should see the texture of the syrup changing and crystals starting to form. Remove from heat and transfer the ginger to the cooling rack in a single layer. When cool and dry, transfer to an airtight container and store in a cool, dark place. Will keep approximately one year.

MIXES & BATTERS

MEXICAN SPICE MIX

1 tsp ground ancho chile
1 tsp ground cinnamon
½ tsp ground ginger
½ tsp ground cloves
½ tsp ground nutmeg
¼ tsp ground cayenne

*Store at room temperature in an airtight
container. Will keep one year.*

SANGRITA

traditional | Jalisco | 1920s

BLEND | CABALLITO | NO ICE

In a blender, combine until smooth:

4 oz orange juice
4 oz lime juice
4 oz apple juice
1 oz pineapple juice
1 oz ginger syrup
1 oz grenadine
2 tsp Mexican Spice Mix
tiny pinch of salt

MAKES 4 SERVINGS

*Serve chilled alongside tequila for side-by-side
sipping.*

BLOODY MARY MIX

Based on Jeffrey Morgenthaler's recipe

In an electric blender, blend until smooth:

2 14.5-oz cans fire-roasted tomatoes

1 small garlic clove

1 quarter avocado

1 oz Worcestershire sauce

³⁄₄ oz lemon juice

1 tsp steak sauce

1 tsp black pepper

1 tsp celery salt

1 tsp hot sauce

¹⁄₂ tsp horseradish

¹⁄₂ tsp chile powder

¹⁄₄ cup water

Keep refrigerated. Will last about one week.

TOM & JERRY BATTER

Based on Andrew Bohrer's recipe

Into two bowls, separate the yolks and whites of:

12 eggs

Combine with egg yolks and beat with an electric mixer until consistent:

1 cup superfine white sugar

1 stick unsalted butter (room temperature)

Beat egg whites to stiff peaks, then gently fold the two mixtures together and add:

1 tsp ground allspice

1 tsp ground cinnamon

1 tsp ground cloves

1 tsp vanilla extract

Keep refrigerated. Will last three days.

HOT BUTTERED RUM BATTER

In a pot over medium-low heat, add:

1 quart vanilla ice cream, softened
4 sticks unsalted butter, softened
1 lb brown sugar
2 tsp cinnamon
1 tsp nutmeg

*Stir until consistent, then pour into an airtight
container and freeze. Batter will keep for over
one year, no problem.*

MEXICAN CHOCOLATE GANACHE

*In a double boiler over medium heat,
melt and stir to combine:*

4 oz dark chocolate
1 cup heavy cream

Whisk in:

6 tbsp cocoa powder
¾ cup demerara sugar

Stir in:

2 tsp Mexican Spice Mix

Keep refrigerated. Will last one year.

TICALOID 210S

Developed by Dave Arnold

Combine:

4 ½ tbsp gum arabic
½ tbsp xanthan gum

*Store at room temperature. Will keep
indefinitely.*

Index

BY FAMILY
SLINGS

SOURS

FORTIFIED WINES

BY BASE
BRANDY

BY OCCASION

BRUNCH

HOT AFTERNOON

BY STRENGTH
HIGH ABV

LOW ABV

RESOURCES

GEAR & GLASSWARE

The Boston Shaker *thebostonshaker.com*

Cocktail Emporium *cocktailemporium.com*

Cocktail Kingdom *cocktailkingdom.com*

Libbey *shop.libbey.com*

Umami Mart *umamimart.com*

ICE

Camper English *alcademics.com*

Tovolo *tovolo.com*

True Cubes *truecubes.com*

MARKET GOODS

Bob's Red Mill *bobsredmill.com*

Di Bruno Bros *dibruno.com*

Mountain Rose Herbs *mountainroseherbs.com*

Oaktown Spice Shop *oaktownspiceshop.com*

The Spice House *thespicehouse.com*

LIQUOR, ETC. *(regional restrictions apply)*

Astor Wines *astorwines.com*

BG Reynolds *bgreynolds.com*

Drizly *drizly.com*

Craftshack *craftshack.com*

Hi-Time *hitimewine.net*

Minibar *minibardelivery.com*

Saucey *saucey.com*

Small Hand Foods *smallhandfoods.com*

Wine.com *wine.com*

FURTHER READING

And a Bottle of Rum, Wayne Curtis

The Bar Book, Jeffrey Morgenthaler

Cocktail Codex, Alex Day, Nick Fauchald
   & David Kaplan

The Drunken Botanist, Amy Stewart

Imbibe!, David Wondrich

The Joy of Mixology, Gary Regan

Meehan's Bartender Manual, Jim Meehan

Moonshine!, Matthew Rowley

The New Craft of the Cocktail, Dale DeGroff

Potions of the Caribbean, Jeff "Beachbum" Berry

A Proper Drink, Robert Simonson

Punch, David Wondrich

Regarding Cocktails, Sasha Petraske

Smuggler's Cove, Martin & Rebecca Cate

Spirit of the Cane, Jared Brown & Anistatia Miller

The Flavor Bible, Karen Page & Andrew Dornenburg

Tiki: Modern Tropical Cocktails, Shannon Mustipher

PUBLICATIONS & WEBSITES

EUVS *euvs-vintage-cocktail-books.cld.bz*

Imbibe *imbibemagazine.com*

Punch *punchdrink.com*

{ COLOPHON }

THIS BOOK WAS DESIGNED AND ILLUSTRATED USING:
PALOMINO BLACKWING 602 PENCILS,
ADOBE INDESIGN, ILLUSTRATOR, AND PHOTOSHOP.
TYPEFACE FAMILIES ARE:
SENTINEL, FUTURA, ROUTER,
CONQUEROR, AND WHITNEY INDEX.
PRINTED IN AUSTIN, TEXAS,
ON ARJOBEX POLYART PAPER.